PSYCHO-THERAPY TO GO

Lillenas Drama

PSYCHO-THERAPY TO GO

Fourteen Mind–Expanding
Comedies and Dramas That Have
Nothing at All to Do with
Sigmund Freud

BY STEVE TROTT

Lillenas PUBLISHING COMPANY

KANSAS CITY, MO 64141

Contents

Let Me Introduce . . .

Here's who you will meet in this collection of short plays:

A confused corpse who discusses with the audience the reason for his demise (theme: bitterness); a troubled woman who discusses with the disembodied speaker-voice at a drive-through restaurant her unexpected pregnancy (theme: sharing burdens); and a woman who discusses the horrible secret of her father's and her past, with the pastor who conducted her father's funeral (theme: child sexual abuse).

In this collection you will experience: the apostle Peter trying to explain to a surprise disciple what happened just before the cock crowed three times (theme: forgiveness); the patriarch Abraham trying to explain to Isaac why there is no lamb for the sacrifice (theme: obeying God); and a forlorn 20th-century father trying to explain to his wife why he is suddenly weeping uncontrollably in the aisle at K-Mart (theme: the empty nest).

You will be introduced to a group of social outcasts who will ask your congregation point blank whether there is room in your church for them (theme: AIDS, addiction, divorce, old age); as well as a group of would-be mothers of some of the most influential people in history, gathered in a waiting room preparing to terminate their pregnancies (theme: sanctity of life).

Finally, you will meet a runaway teenager whose phone calls home to her mother reveal experiences remarkably similar to those of the prodigal son (theme: parent-teen relationships).

Psychotherapy to Go ✓

Theme

Bearing others' burdens; talking out our problems

Tone

Humorous

Cast

VOICE: *of woman in her 40s*
JOYCE: *in her 30s, pregnant*

Scene

The drive-through lane at a fast-food restaurant

Props

Front car seat (or two chairs placed side by side)
Speaker (the kind used in drive-through restaurants)

Costumes

Modern

Production Notes

It is possible to perform this sketch without a drive-through speaker; JOYCE pretending to speak through the car window is sufficient. However, it is important that the offstage VOICE be electronically amplified to produce the desired drive-through restaurant effect.

Summary

A woman with an unexpected pregnancy finds solace in a heart-to-heart talk with the Voice coming out of the speaker at a fast-food restaurant.

(As scene opens Joyce *is sitting on the driver's side of a car seat, facing audience, looking to her right at a real or imaginary fast-food restaurant speaker.)*

Voice: Hi! Welcome to McWendiking. May I take your order?

Joyce: Just a minute, please. I'm not through checking the menu.

Voice: Hi! Welcome to McWendiking. May I take your order?

Joyce: I said just a minute, I'm not— Never mind.

(She crawls across car seat to passenger side, leans out imaginary window. When she next speaks, her mouth will be inches from the speaker.)

Voice: Welcome to McWendiking. May I take—

Joyce: I'm not through reading the menu!

Voice: Oh—well—whenever you're ready then.

Joyce *(sarcastically):* Thank you.

Voice: Uh, excuse me, ma'am. I can see you from my window station. Are you coming through *backward?*

*(*Joyce *turns and waves sheepishly toward imaginary pay window behind her.)*

Joyce: Hi.

Voice: First time in a drive-through?

Joyce: No, I . . . just can't get my driver-side door closed.

Voice: It looks closed from here, ma'am.

Joyce: Well, yes. I mean from the inside. The hinges—you have to lift up on the door while you close it to make it latch. I can only do it from the outside—standing up, you know? So I have to crawl in from the passenger side. It's not pretty, believe me.

Voice: This is a drive-through, honey. All you need to do is open the window.

Joyce: Well, that's nice in theory, but I also have the added luxury of an electric window that doesn't work.

Voice: Bummer.

Joyce: Yeah, I was pressing the button to lower it one day and all of a sudden smoke started pouring out. I thought, I'd better get this thing rolled up before the motor burns out or I'm gonna have rain, sleet, snow, and the gloom of night all over my lap. So now it's rolled up—permanently. Or at least till I can come up with a hundred and twenty-five bucks for a new window motor.

VOICE: Cars are expensive.

JOYCE: You can say that again.

VOICE: So—why didn't you just come inside and order?

JOYCE: Because then I'd have to crawl all the way across the stupid seat again—

VOICE: Isn't that what you did anyway?

(JOYCE *considers her situation for a moment, sighs wearily.*)

JOYCE: You know, I haven't been thinking too clearly, lately. *(Rubs her forehead)* Not a lotta sleep this past week.

VOICE: Sounds like you better get that door fixed.

JOYCE: Yeah, well, the money's a little short right now. In fact, I couldn't even drive the thing for the last month because we couldn't afford a new muffler till payday. I had to get the kids ready for school an hour early every day, drive my husband in his car 30 minutes to work, then drop the kids off on the way back.

VOICE: So you have kids.

JOYCE: Two and a half.

VOICE: Two and a half years old, that can be a tough age.

(JOYCE *looks down at her large stomach, rubs it.*)

JOYCE: No. Two and a half kids. We're trying to keep up with the national average.

VOICE: I get it. You've got one on the way, huh?

JOYCE: *In* the way is more like it. Yeah, any day now. I can't wait. Between the back pain, the humidity, sleepless nights—I'm going crazy. I almost lost it completely this morning.

VOICE: What happened?

JOYCE: Oh, some truck driver nearly drove me off the road. Ran me into a ditch.

VOICE: Men! They think they own the highway.

JOYCE: Well, I didn't catch the gender, but whoever it was I let 'em have it.

VOICE: Way to go! Wha'd you do? Cut him off, flip him off, tell him off?

JOYCE: No, none of those. Not exactly.

VOICE: Well, what else *is* there?

JOYCE: Actually, I . . . washed my windows at 'em.

VOICE: You did *what?*

JOYCE: I washed my windows?

VOICE: No comprendo.

JOYCE: Well, you remember I said I've been driving my husband's car for the last month—

VOICE: Yeah.

JOYCE: He's got an old T-bird and the horn is at the end of the turn signal lever, believe it or not.

VOICE: OK.

JOYCE: But now I'm back in my own car where the tip of the turn signal lever is the window washer button.

VOICE: Uh-huh.

JOYCE: So, I went to lay on the horn and I . . . laid on the Windex instead.

VOICE: Weird.

JOYCE: Housewife through and through, I guess. There I am, heading into a ditch on the verge of meeting my Maker and I'm washing windows.

VOICE: Crazy.

JOYCE: Well, you know what they say. Cleanliness is next to godliness.

VOICE: So I've heard.

JOYCE: So here I am. I avoided the ditch, got all the bugs off the windshield, and now I'm sitting backward telling my life story to somebody I've not only never met, but never even seen. Reminds me of going to confession.

VOICE: Going where?

JOYCE: Confession. I grew up Catholic. We used to have to go into this little closet and confess our sins to a screen.

VOICE: Oh. I grew up Baptist, myself. We never sinned.

JOYCE: Must be nice.

VOICE: Well, depends on how you look at it.

JOYCE: They say that confession is good for the soul.

VOICE: Well, we all need to talk, you know. Keeps us from going nuts.

JOYCE: Yeah.

VOICE: So what can I get you for lunch?

JOYCE (*after a moment*): I didn't want it, you know.

VOICE: Well, it's just past 11:00. I might be able to get you a breakfast, let me check.

JOYCE: The baby I mean.

VOICE: Pardon me?

JOYCE: I'm not so sure I want another child.

VOICE (*comprehending*): Ah.

JOYCE: I mean, it's not the best time right now. Things aren't going very well between John and me. I think it's a lot to do with money. He was laid off a couple of years ago and what he's doing now isn't what he feels is him, you know what I mean?

VOICE (*with compassion, understanding*): I think so.

JOYCE: And we already have two, you know? Old enough to be left on their own once in a while. I had these big plans to go back to school in a couple more years, get my degree. We weren't planning on this, it wasn't what we wanted. I mean we're short enough on money as it is, you know? And about the only thing, if I want to help out at all, the only thing I'm qualified for is to work at a drive-through restaurant. That's not very fulfilling to me somehow.

VOICE: I hear you.

JOYCE: Oh my goodness, I'm so sorry. I didn't mean—

VOICE: That's OK.

JOYCE: This is so embarrassing.

VOICE: Hey, I understand.

JOYCE: I'm glad I'm facing the wrong direction. I think I'll just drive out the back entrance and move to Oregon.

(*She begins crawling back across the car seat.*)

VOICE: I have five children myself.

(*She stops crawling back across the car seat.*)

JOYCE: You do?

VOICE: Eighteen, 17, 16, 15 . . . and 3.

JOYCE: Woops.

VOICE: Yeah, woops is right.

JOYCE *(carefully, after a few moments):* Did you even think about—I mean, when you first found out, did you ever consider—?

VOICE: I said I was a Baptist, remember?

JOYCE: Oh, that's right.

VOICE *(changing her tone):* Yeah, I thought about it. I mean, I was already raising four kids on my own, you know.

JOYCE: But I thought—

VOICE: My husband left me 13 years ago.

JOYCE: Oh. *(Thinks a moment)* But what about—

VOICE: The three-year-old?

JOYCE: Yes.

VOICE: Well, remember what I said about Baptists not sinning?

JOYCE: Uh-huh.

VOICE: I lied.

(She begins chuckling, is joined by JOYCE. *Their chuckles turn into outright laughter, brought on by the relief of tension.)*

JOYCE: We shouldn't be laughing about this.

VOICE: Well, you know what they say—

JOYCE: What?

VOICE: Confession is good for the soul.

(They laugh some more, then JOYCE *begins crying softly.)*

JOYCE: So how's that three-year-old doing?

VOICE: He's beautiful. Wouldn't be the same without him.

*(*JOYCE *reaches for her purse and takes out one used tissue and dabs her eyes with it.)*

JOYCE: I think I'm ready to order now.

VOICE: Fire away, honey.

JOYCE: Just a couple of napkins, please. I need to blow my nose.

(The Voice *breaks into friendly laughter again;* Joyce *joins in despite her tears.)*

Voice: Tell you what. I'm due to go on my lunch break any second now anyway. How 'bout if I treat and the two of us can talk a little more, face-to-face.

Joyce: Your treat? No, I couldn't.

Voice: You sure could.

Joyce: But you don't even know me. Why would you want to buy me lunch?

Voice: Hey, for someone who doesn't know you, you sure did a whole lot o' confessing just now.

Joyce: Old habits die hard, I guess.

Voice: Tell me about it. Now wha' d'ya say to that lunch?

Joyce: Well, all right. But I can pay for mine.

Voice: How 'bout if you get it the next time.

Joyce: OK, sure. I'll be right in.

Voice: *In,* wha' d'you mean, *in?*

Joyce: I thought you said—

Voice: Honey, I said I'd buy you lunch. I didn't say anything about eating *here.* Now you slide over and drive that thing you call a car up to the door and pick me up. We're going down the road to a *real* restaurant.

(A relaxed smile breaks across Joyce's *face.)*

Joyce: I can live with that.

Voice: Be with you in half a minute.

Joyce: Roger. Over and out.

Voice: Over and out.

*(*Joyce *slides back into the driver's side. She sighs quietly, glances down, and strokes her stomach gently. Her smile lingers as the lights fade out.)*

A Mountain in Moriah:
A Play for Two Voices

Theme

Obeying God no matter the cost

Scriptural Background

Genesis 22:1-12

Tone

Serious

Cast

NARRATOR: *male or female; reads a condensed version of Genesis 22:1-10 at play's beginning, and verses 11 and 12 at play's end (NASB)*

ABRAHAM: *male; an old man, father to Isaac*

ISAAC: *male or female (Because this is a readers theatre presentation, the audience will find it acceptable that a woman play the part of Isaac. Her lighter voice will convey the sense of a boy or teenager, while her maturity will provide the emotional depth and vocal expression necessary to this role—qualities that might be lacking should the part be played by someone whose age and gender are more identifiable as Isaac.)*

Scene

A mountaintop. If done as a readers theatre, no scenery is needed.

Props

Knife
Firewood

Fire pot

If done as a readers theatre, all props can be mimed.

Costumes

Biblical. Or if done as readers theatre, dark clothing.

Summary

When Isaac confronts Abraham about the absence of a lamb for their mountaintop sacrifice, Abraham must try to find the right words to explain to his son that he, Isaac, has been designated by God to be the sacrifice on this occasion.

NARRATOR: "Now it came about after these things that God tested Abraham, and said to him, 'Abraham . . . take now your son, your only son, whom you love, Isaac, and go to the land of Moriah; and offer him there as a burnt offering on one of the mountains of which I will tell you.' So Abraham . . . arose and went to the place of which God had told him. On the third day Abraham raised his eyes and saw the place from a distance. . . . And Abraham took the wood of the burnt offering and laid it on Isaac his son, and he took in his hand the fire and the knife. So the two of them walked on together. And Isaac spoke to Abraham . . . and he said, 'Behold, the fire and the wood, but where is the lamb for the burnt offering?' And Abraham said, 'God will provide for Himself the lamb for the burnt offering, my son.' So the two of them walked on together. Then they came to the place of which God had told him; and Abraham . . . bound his son Isaac, and . . . stretched out his hand, and took the knife to slay his son."

(The actors portraying ABRAHAM *and* ISAAC *may already be in place onstage, at podiums or holding scripts, or can enter individually,* ISAAC *miming carrying the wood and then setting it down,* ABRAHAM *miming carrying a fire pot and knife and then setting them down.)*

ISAAC *(looking around):* So, Papa—where is this lamb that you told me God would provide?

ABRAHAM: We must be patient, Isaac. God is never in a hurry when we are in a rush.

ISAAC: But we have come all this way to offer a sacrifice, and there is no sacrifice in sight! *(Animated)* We have the wood that *I* carried. We have the fire that *you* carried. We even have, thank God, the knife that you kept dropping along the way.

17

ABRAHAM (*setting knife down*): Yes, my hands seem to be slippery today—

ISAAC: I think if this lamb from God ever *does* show up, my father had better allow his son to do the honors. For your hands are not only slippery today—they are downright unsteady.

ABRAHAM (*almost to himself*): It is my heart that is unsteady, not my hands.

ISAAC (*lightly*): I think my father is getting old.

ABRAHAM: Your father was *already* old when he begot you.

ISAAC (*sighs*): The miracle child.

ABRAHAM: Yes. The miracle child.

ISAAC (*looking around again*): But no miraculous lamb—

ABRAHAM: Isaac, do you remember the story about Yahweh calling me to leave my home in Haran and follow Him to a land that He would show me?

ISAAC: Yes, Papa.

ABRAHAM: And how, even though I was afraid, I went out not knowing where I was going?

ISAAC: How could I forget? It is your second favorite story.

ABRAHAM (*lost in thought*): Yes. My second favorite.

ISAAC: So?

ABRAHAM: Hmmm?

ISAAC: So what about this story? The call of God to my papa.

ABRAHAM: Yes. Well, it seems that God has called to your papa again—

ISAAC (*sensing adventure*): Another journey not-knowing-where?

ABRAHAM (*somber*): No. This time it is a journey not-knowing-how.

ISAAC (*beat*): I don't understand.

ABRAHAM: It is this one, Isaac. This journey today to a mountain in Moriah.

ISAAC (*lightly*): Papa, this is not a journey not-knowing-how. Except for finding your invisible lamb, the "how" is easy: we climb, we build a fire, we offer up a sacrifice. Simple as that! I could do it blindfolded with my hands tied behind my back!

ABRAHAM (*erupting*): There will be no blindfold! Your hands will not be bound!

ISAAC (*stunned*): Well of course, Papa—I was only joking.

ABRAHAM *(recovering):* Your name means laughter. I suppose it is only fitting that you should joke at such a time as this.

ISAAC: Such a time as what? A simple sacrifice, Papa. Don't make a mountain out of a molehill!

ABRAHAM: What God has this time called me to is neither simple . . . nor small.

ISAAC: Mama is right. You take things too seriously. God asked you to offer up a sacrifice, not lay down your life.

ABRAHAM: No. Not *my* life. *(Beat)* Your life.

ISAAC *(beat):* *My* life. *(Points to himself, trying to inject humor)* The lamb of Moriah: is I-ah?

ABRAHAM: You can still joke—

ISAAC: I am joking in the hopes that *you* are joking. You *are* joking, aren't you? *(Silence)* You are not. Then call me Isaac no more, for I no longer laugh.

ABRAHAM *(searching for words):* I can imagine your shock—

ISAAC *(interrupting):* When were you going to tell me! What were you going to do, wait until the fire was blazing, then shove me on it? Wait for my back to be turned, then crush my skull with a rock? Or was it going to be face-to-face, your knife hidden in your sleeve—

ABRAHAM: I was searching for the right words—

ISAAC: Believe me, Father, there *are* no *right* words. Every word you could possibly come up with would be precisely the wrong word. There is only one possible correct word you could speak to me at this moment.

ABRAHAM: And that word is—

ISAAC: Live. *(Beat)* Live. *(Softer)* Live.

ABRAHAM *(his loyalty torn):* It is the one word I am forbidden.

ISAAC *(realizing ABRAHAM's resolve):* Then say nothing. Just—turn back. We will descend the mountain the way we came.

ABRAHAM: To go backward is to say no to God. I learned many years ago that the direction of one's footsteps is the truest and most accurate voice of the soul. Isaac, I *cannot* go back.

ISAAC: You are strong in the faith.

ABRAHAM: I am long in the faith.

ISAAC: And have you been long enough in the faith to believe God's deceptions?

ABRAHAM: He has always kept His word.

ISAAC: He changed your name to Abraham: "Father of a multitude."

ABRAHAM: A rough translation, yes.

ISAAC: Can your God supply for you a multitude from my dead body?

ABRAHAM: He is *your* God too.

ISAAC: Believe me, my devotion is being severely tested at the moment!

ABRAHAM: When Sarah's body was as good as dead, she gave birth to a baby boy—

ISAAC *(interrupting)*: Who was led by his father to a mountain in Moriah.

ABRAHAM: Do you think I would not lay down my life without a second thought, without one—final glance at Sarah, without—one last breath, if it meant that you might live? My only consolation is that the God who on the occasion of your conception brought you forth from the dead, might now, on the occasion of your—

ISAAC: Murder?

ABRAHAM *(defeated)*: Might bring you back from death itself.

ISAAC: A noble concept, Papa. If only God will act according to your notions of nobility.

ABRAHAM *(distant)*: He acts as He acts. He does what He does. He chooses what He chooses. And we—I—have no choice but to respond accordingly.

ISAAC *(lighter again, becoming submissive)*: Perhaps your response could come more slowly, say 10 or 20 years from now.

ABRAHAM: Walking in—

ISAAC: Yes, I know: Walking in obedience to God does not include the dragging of one's feet.

ABRAHAM: You have learned your lessons well, my son.

ISAAC *(beat, respectfully)*: You have *lived* well, my father. *(Pause, then subdued)* Tell me, Papa, when you are rushing to obey God's orders, do you ever wonder if the voice is real?

ABRAHAM *(quietly)*: It is the exact same voice that spoke the promises that have since come true. *(Beat, takes ISAAC's hands)* The greatest of those was you.

ISAAC: Was.

ABRAHAM: Is.

ISAAC *(beat)*: Was. *(Pause, pulls hands away)* Good-bye, Papa.

ABRAHAM: You are leaving?

ISAAC: No. I am lying down. Offer up the sacrifice—and hurry.

ABRAHAM: You are telling me—to answer God in the affirmative?

ISAAC: Have you not already given Him such an answer in your heart?

ABRAHAM: My yes has been on my tongue, but my fingertips are slow of speech. Three days ago, when we began our journey to Moriah, I was uncertain what my answer ultimately would be.

ISAAC: But the direction of your feet—was toward the mountaintop.

ABRAHAM: My faith—moves me forward.

ISAAC: Toward yes.

ABRAHAM: Toward the affirmative.

ISAAC: You are *always* moving toward the affirmative, Papa. It is the constant posture of your life: bowing before God and following after.

ABRAHAM: Is it not, in the end, our only alternative?

ISAAC: Saying yes to God—

ABRAHAM: Yes.

ISAAC: Yes.

ABRAHAM: Yes. *(Mimes picking up knife)*

ISAAC *(after a bit):* Papa.

ABRAHAM: Speak, my one and only son, my laughter—

ISAAC: It might be wise, after all, to tie my hands behind my back, lest, at the final moment, my stubborn will to live should rise up and defend itself against the will of God that I should die. For I suspect it is no easy thing: to make oneself a living sacrifice to God. *(Holds hands out to be bound)*

ABRAHAM *(barely able to speak):* No easy thing at all. *(Mimes tying hands)*

ISAAC: Then you have been there, too, yourself, and survived?

ABRAHAM: No, my son. I go there now—with you.

(He mimes lifting the knife as ISAAC *bows his head; they freeze in this position as* NARRATOR *reads from Genesis 22:11-12.)*

NARRATOR: "But the angel of the LORD called to him from heaven, and said, 'Abraham . . . Do not stretch out your hand against the lad, and do nothing to him; for now I know that you fear God, since you have not withheld your son, your only son, from Me.'"

(Lights fade out.)

Prodi-Gal ✓

Theme

Mother-daughter relationships; runaway teens

Tone

Serious, but lighthearted

Cast

GIRL: *in her late teens*

Scene

A variety of locations suggested by a chair, a box, a cot, etc.

Props

Variety of telephones, including pay phone and car phone
Sweet roll
Wallet with credit cards
Easy chair
Cigarette, ashtray
Cardboard box
Drink in glass
Chair (representing car seat)
Purse
Birthday card in envelope
Gum
Cot
Small table or desk
Coffee mug

Optional Sound Effects

Bus terminal ambiance
Rock music
Car engine
Rain

Costumes

Modern teen

Production Notes

You may wish, in Scene 5, to have the girl appear to be eight months pregnant. Also, director should make sure that there is an adequate pause between each new line of the daughter's monologue to indicate that she is listening to what her mother is saying (or trying to say) on the other end of the telephone.

Summary

Through a series of brief telephone calls home to her mother, the audience is able to trace the adventures of a runaway teenager. She begins carefree, as did the prodigal son, but ends up much as he did: down on her luck and longing for home. And for her mom.

Scene 1

(A teenage GIRL *stands at a pay phone, taking a bite out of a sweet roll while waiting for someone on the other end to answer. If sound effects are being employed—bus terminal. The* GIRL's *opening lines are continually interrupted by her anxious mother, whose voice is never heard by the audience.)*

Yeah, Mom. This is—

Yes, I'm—

No, I wasn't in an ac—

No, I haven't been—

No, I'm not in—

Mom, just *relax*. I haven't been mugged, drugged, arrested, molested, kidnapped, or handicapped. I'm not in jail, I'm not in the hospital, I'm not even in trouble.

Well, yeah—except with you.

For Pete's sake, Mother, the *sun* is coming up. How could I not realize it's past my curfew!

(She looks around at imaginary terminal.)

Well, I'm in a bus depot over on—

(Getting testy) What I'm doing in a bus depot is grabbing a sweet roll and giving you a call to let you know that I won't be home for breakfast.

(Sighs) What it means is . . . Mom, listen, there's something I have to tell you.

No, I'm not pregnant. *(Rolls her eyes)*

Mom, will you just settle down for a second? This isn't the easiest thing I've ever had to say, you know?

OK. OK. I'll tell you. *(Hesitates)* Remember how Dad is always saying: It's my way or the highway?

(Testier) Well, he says it a *lot*. Mom, will you just listen? He always—sometimes—when he's upset, he says: It's my way or the highway. OK? Well—I've decided on the highway.

Wha' d'you mean, wha' do I mean? I'm calling from a bus depot telling you I decided on the highway. Figure it out, Mother! You watch *Wheel of Fortune*. Sheesh, wha' do I mean!

(Looks around again; speaks more quietly)

I don't know. One-ninety-six, I guess.

(Looks around again, rolls her eyes)

South. Look, Mom, that's not the point—

Mom, it doesn't matter which highway—

No, you're not coming to get—

Mom, the bus is leaving in five minutes. You'll never make it.

School is overrated anyway. Look, I'll call you when I get there, all right?

I don't know, wherever I end up.

(Softens as she hears her mother crying)

Listen, don't. No, please, Mom, don't do that, come on.

Mom, I'll call you, OK?

Mom, good-bye.

(*She hangs up the phone, then takes out her mother's wallet, let's plastic strip of credit cards cascade downward.*)

Take a look in your purse. You won't feel like crying then.

(*Lights fade out.*)

Scene 2

(*Lights fade in on GIRL sitting in an easy chair, a cigarette in one hand. She is already engaged in a telephone conversation.*)

Hey, it's not like I left you penniless. You've still got your Shell card.

I know you could.

I knew you wouldn't.

Because you'd never do that.

Because your kid could be on trial for murdering Santa Claus and you'd not only be protesting her innocence daily outside the Supreme Court, but you'd be up late each night making peanut butter cookies to take to her in prison.

(*Softening*) Because that's the way you are.

(*Swallows*) You're welcome.

Mom, come on, don't.

(*Sighs, toys with her cigarette*)

Well, remember Melissa?

Yeah, [name of distant city]. I'm with her. But just for a while, so don't get any ideas—

No, she quit smoking.

(*Looks at cigarette in her hand*)

Yeah, I know secondhand smoke is dangerous. Mom, she quit smoking right after she moved down here, OK? So quit worrying.

(*Puts cigarette out in ashtray*)

Her folks think I'm on spring break.

Yeah, I know it's October. They're extremely gullible people.

(Giving in) All right, they went to Europe.

Yeah, a business trip. I'm staying here till I can find my own place.

I'll get a job, OK? Don't worry. I gotta go. I just wanted to let you know I got here OK.

(She hangs up. Lights fade out quickly.)

Scene 3

(Lights fade in on GIRL *sitting on floor next to a cardboard box. Phone is on floor next to her. In her free hand is a mixed drink, which she sips occasionally. Sound effects, if used, rock music.)*

Hi—Mom?

(To offstage friends) Hey! Turn it down, you guys!

(She laughs; music doesn't change.)

We're just having a little housewarming celebration.

Yeah, me and Melissa got our own place.

What's that? I can't hear you—

My phone number?

(Glances at phone, sees number, ignores it)

No, it's not there. *(Shouts off)* Hey, anybody know our phone number?

(Giddy) I'm not even sure we know the address. Listen, I'll send it to you first thing in the morning, OK?

The street address and the phone address—whatever.

Listen, Mom, I gotta go. My friends are calling me.

What?

Mom, I can't hear you. Send me a letter or something—

Bye.

(Her final word is spoken with her mouth a foot or two away from the mouthpiece as she is already hanging up the phone. She looks around on the floor for her glass, which is right in front of her.)

All right, you guys. Who stole my drink?

(Lights fade out.)

Scene 4

(In the darkness we have the GIRL *singing her opening line. Lights come up on her sitting in a chair wearing a jacket. She is speaking into a car phone. Sound effects: car engine, highway.)*

Happy birthday, dear Mom, happy birthday to you! Guess who?

Yup! Thought I'd surprise you and wish you a happy birthday a couple days early.

Guess where I'm calling from!

Nope. Cruisin' down Interstate 55 in a brand-new Miata.

(Rolls her eyes) No, it's not mine. It's Eric's.

(She turns toward imaginary driver's seat and smiles toward an invisible boyfriend.)

Oh, just a guy I met. Hey, did you get my card?

You're kidding. I sent it three days ago. Stupid post office.

(Looks down at her lap, slightly annoyed)

Yes, I'm wearing my seatbelt. *(Changes subject)* So, you guys doing anything special for your birthday?

That's a nice restaurant. Why'd he take you *last* weekend? *(In disbelief)* Last Thursday?

I thought—what's your birthday then?

The 9th? I thought it was the 19th! Oh well, the card will be even later than I thought it was going to be.

(She laughs, a bit uneasy.)

Yes, I know I never sent you my address.

And phone number.

At least I remembered your birthday.

Yeah, I think there's a return address on the envelope.

What?

(To driver) I think we just drove out of range or something. She got cut off.

(Listens as he says something to her)

No, don't turn around.

(She hangs up phone, begins digging in purse.)

I need some gum. Talking to her makes my mouth dry.

(*Pulls out bent birthday card in envelope*)

What—my mom's birthday card. I musta never even mailed it.

(*Shoves it back in purse*)

Oh well, she doesn't like being reminded of how old she is anyway.

(*Flashes driver a smile; finds gum*)

Want some gum?

(*Lights fade out as engine roars.*)

Scene 5

(*In the darkness, the phone is ringing. Lights fade up on* GIRL *sleeping on a cot. She slowly wakes, gains some degree of semiconsciousness, rises to answer phone, which is on a small table or desk across the room. When* GIRL *speaks, it is sleepily, perhaps drugged.*)

Hello—?

(*Sniffs*) Yes, this is . . . Mom?

(*She is suddenly alert. And self-conscious.*)

How did you know where to call?

Melissa? Oh, yeah, I ran into her a couple o' days ago. I musta mentioned where I was working or something.

Yeah, no, it's a good job. I . . . really like it.

Eric?

(*A noticeable change comes over her.*)

No, I haven't seen Eric since—well, I don't know. Maybe five or six months now.

No, everything's fine. Why?

I'm, no, you just caught me sleeping in. (*Sniffs*) I've had a little cold lately, so I took a sick day to rest up.

No, I'll be fine.

(*She looks around the room; lies.*)

Yeah, it's a nice place. Really, it's a good job.

28

(She suddenly screams and jumps up on table or chair, staring wildly at something moving across the floor. After a bit she regains her equilibrium enough to speak again.)

Nothing. Nothing. Just, a hornet landed on my arm, that's all. Scared me there for a second.

No, really, it was just a hornet. There's a little hole in the screen. I talked to the landlord, he said he'd fix it.

It's no big deal, Mom. I'm sure he's going to fix it. He's a really nice old man. He's really good at fixing things. He probably just forgot, you know?

OK, I'll remind him again. Listen, I've gotta go, I'm gonna be late for work.

Bye.

(She hangs up. She's still sitting up on the chair or desk. Now she curls up into a fetal position, frightened and tearful.)

I *hate* rats! I *hate rats*! I hate my *life!* Oh, *God*, I hate my life!

(Lights slowly fade out.)

Scene 6

(Sound effects if used: rainfall. Lights fade in on GIRL sitting on a living room chair sipping a cup of coffee. A telephone sits on a small table beside her. Her hair is damp, as though she has been out in the rain. After a few moments she speaks to an imaginary woman. Her manner throughout scene is humble and repentant.)

Yeah, I suppose you're right. No use putting it off any longer.

(Puts mug down on table and picks up phone. She dials zero.)

Yes, I'd like to place a collect call. Eight-one-five, two-three-five-seven.

Just say . . . your daughter.

(While she waits for operator to make the call, she closes her eyes and takes a deep breath, then sighs a long sigh.)

(Quietly) Hi.

(She listens for a few moments as her mother responds.)

(Still quiet.) Yes, I'm fine. I—

Just a few hours south of you. I was—

Mom, don't cry, please. I know it's been a long—

(Waits again, listening; fighting tears)

29

I was hitchhiking, and they let me off in the rain. Wet out there.

I know it's not safe, but I didn't have any—

They were decent people. *(Glances toward imaginary woman)* Anyway, this really nice lady saw me standing on the road outside her house and invited me to come in out of—

(Embarrassed) Yeah, nothing at all. Maybe a buck or two in change.

Today? *(Looks at coffee)* I don't know, a cup of coffee. Oh, and an apple this morning. There was this tree right by the road—

I'm in a house just off the highway. They have a big farm. It's very pretty. Nice to be back in this part of the country again.

Don't be crazy, Mom. It's gotta be a four-hour trip.

No, listen. If you'll wire me the money—just enough for the bus—I'll pay you back as soon as I can get a job.

No, really, I mean it. There's a bus leaving later today. I'll take the first job that's open. I'll work overtime and weekends. I'm going to pay back every—

(Glances toward woman) I don't know. It's an old road that runs parallel with the Interstate. *(Listens to woman)* Highway 37.

(She covers the mouthpiece and talks to imaginary woman.)

She wants to talk to you. She wants to see if she can reimburse you for a hot meal and some warm clothes. But it's not necessary, really.

(Mimes handing the phone to imaginary woman, then stops. As she delivers her final two lines, we sense in her voice and manner a combination of relief, a sense of peace, and the beginnings of restoration.)

And she's going to ask for directions. She's . . . coming to take me home.

(Extends phone toward imaginary woman as lights slowly fade to black)

Leave and Let Leave ✓

Theme

The empty nest; parenting

Tone

Humorous

Cast

TED: *a man in his late 30s or 40s*
ANN: *his wife, of similar age*

Scene

K-Mart or similar store. Empty stage will do.

Props

Box of tissues
Shopping list
Bedspread
Shopping cart full of a variety of "school supplies" as described in script (not all items mentioned need be visible; pillows and towels can give the appearance of a full shopping cart)

Costumes

Modern

Summary

A father is caught emotionally off guard while helping his wife shop for "school supplies" prior to their oldest daughter's departure for college. In the middle of K-Mart he begins weeping, suddenly overwhelmed by what her leaving home really means.

(As sketch opens a woman pushes an overflowing shopping cart across the stage while glancing at a shopping list in her hand. Her husband enters opposite carrying a box of tissues; he waves, crosses to her.)

TED: Honey? Honey! I found the tissues. *(Holds up box)*

ANN *(good-naturedly)*: Where in the world have you *been?* You've been gone for nearly an hour.

TED: Oh, I got sidetracked for a few minutes in the hardware department.

ANN: That's what we figured. I just sent Kimberly to look for you there.

TED *(sees overflowing cart)*: What is *all this!*

ANN: All what?

TED *(dumbfounded)*: You said she needed a few *school* supplies.

ANN: Well, we can't have her going off to college without necessities—

TED: *Necessities!* This looks like she's moving into a . . . a home of her *own.*

ANN: Well, she *is,* sort of. A dormitory.

TED: Let me see that list. *(Grabs it, reads)*

ANN: Just, please don't make any of your this-is-going-to-cost-as-much-as-tuition comments, OK?

TED *(looking at list)*: This isn't going to cost as much as tuition.

ANN: Thank you.

TED *(woefully)*: It's going to cost *more* than tuition. Much, *much* more.

ANN *(good-naturedly)*: Oh, stop it. This is a very special time for her, and I want to make it the best of times.

TED *(grieving over list)*: It was the best of times, it was the worst of times.

ANN: You can quote Charles Dickens all you want, but this is our first child to go away to college, and I'm entitled as a mother to go a bit overboard.

TED *(still reading)*: That would explain the lifeboat you've got listed here.

ANN: *Lifeboat?* Give me that! *(Takes list, reads)* That's *Lifebuoy.* It's soap for your shower. We're almost out, and I knew by the time we got home from shopping you'd be all hot and bothered.

(She laughs; he joins her, then takes list back.)

TED *(reads):* Desk lamp, deodorant, towels, washcloths, pillows, bedding, popcorn popper, shampoo, paper plates, bathroom rug, bedspread, flower vase, wastebasket, toothbrush cup, soap dish, computer paper, surge protector . . . and *Kleenex* tissues! *(Raises box as though proud of his contribution)* That's me!

ANN *(looking at box):* Oh, that's not going to work at all.

TED: Not going to work! What's there not to work about it? It's a box of tissues. You open it, pull one out, and blow your nose!

ANN *(as though she's clarifying the issue):* It's not burgundy.

TED: Burgundy! Why does it have to be burgundy?

ANN: Because there wasn't anything left in teal.

TED: *What?*

ANN *(sheepish):* We've developed a sort of color scheme—

TED: *Color scheme!* It's *Kleenex,* for Pete's sake! Who *cares* what color it is! *(Looking at box)* Just so nobody else has used it!

ANN: Ted. It's a woman's thing, OK? Everything has to be color-coordinated. Please, just go back and see if they have something that will match. Here, take this bedspread as a sample. *(Hands him bedspread)* I'm going to check over this list and make sure we haven't forgotten anything. *(Begins reading)*

TED *(leaving):* Only the lifeboat.

ANN: Pardon me?

TED: You forgot the lifeboat.

ANN *(absorbed in her list):* Yes, well, if you see one on your way to the tissue aisle, pick one out for us, OK? Burgundy.

TED *(muttering to himself):* A woman's thing.

(As ANN looks over her list, TED crosses away from her, then stops and looks down at the bedspread in his hands. His shoulders sag, and he begins weeping quietly. After a few moments of this, he opens tissue box and removes a tissue to wipe his eyes and nose. ANN, meanwhile, suddenly remembers something.)

ANN *(to herself):* Oh, I had a coupon for that. *(She digs in purse, then pulls out coupon, turns to follow TED.)* Ted— *(Sees him stopped in middle of store, approaches)* Ted? *(He turns toward her, sniffles, stuffs tissue in pocket, clears throat.)* I forgot, I have a coupon, we can get one box free if we buy two at the regular price—*(It suddenly strikes her what is happening.)* What are you doing here?

TED (*covering*): Nothing.

ANN: You're standing in the middle of K-Mart staring at a bedspread. I know you have trouble coordinating colors, but it's not anything to be *afraid* of. (*Notices open box*) Why did you open the tissue box that you were going to exchange?

TED: Because I didn't want to wipe my nose on the bedspread. I know how much you hate it when I use my sleeve.

ANN (*bewildered*): Why would you want to wipe your nose on a bedspread? I haven't even removed the price tag yet.

TED (*passionately*): She's gone. My daughter's gone.

ANN: She's not gone. She just went to look for you in the hardware section.

TED: No. I mean *gone*. She's *leaving* us. She's all grown up and she's *leaving* us.

ANN: What are you talking about? She's 18. She's going to college on the other side of town. Thirty-two and a half minutes away.

TED: You don't understand. Something has changed here. (*Looking at bedspread*) It didn't hit me till I was carrying *this*. She won't be sleeping in her *bed* anymore. My oldest daughter, who has been sleeping in that room for her entire life. I used to tell her stories in that room, stories I would make up and that would amaze me that I could make them up, and she would fall asleep in the middle of them and I was always relieved because I never knew for sure whether or not I'd be able to figure out an ending, other than "they all lived happily ever after." (*With bitter realization*) Except not in the same house. (*Sighs*) We used to look in on her before we'd go to bed. Remember how she had that funny way of getting twisted around on top of the blankets and I'd have to pick her up while you rearranged the bedding and then we'd tuck her in all over again? Or how when she was a little older we'd see her underneath the covers with her flashlight, trying to finish reading her latest mystery novel way past bedtime? (*Looks at bedspread in his hands*) Now our daughter needs a *new* bedspread. A new bedspread for a new bed in a new bedroom in a new . . . home.

ANN (*tenderly*): She'll be back every weekend. (*Chuckling*) And if the food in the cafeteria is bad enough, she'll probably be back every night for supper.

TED (*realizing the truth*): No. No, she won't. She'll be back, but it won't be the same. It will never be the same again. (*Takes a breath; there is a moment or two of silence.*) Come on. Let's go get that box of tissues. I hear they've got a great deal going on: buy a new bedspread, get a free box of *Kleenex* to match.

ANN: No, silly. That's only if you buy the lifeboat.

(*They exit arm in arm as lights fade out.*)

Unfamiliar Country: Fear of the Future

Theme

Walking by faith

Scriptural Background

Genesis 12:1; Hebrews 11:8

Tone

Lighthearted but serious

Cast

ABRAHAM: *an old man*
NARRATOR: *reads two Bible verses before monologue begins*

Scene

Empty stage

Costumes

Traditional Old Testament

Production Note

You may wish to have the actor playing Abraham speak in a manner similar to Tevye in *Fiddler on the Roof*.

Summary

Abraham has been called by God to go "out, not knowing where he was going." He reflects in a brief monologue on the difficulty involved in stepping out in faith when he is used to standing firmly on familiar ground. Originally written for a church service kicking off plans to move ahead with a new construction project.

NARRATOR: The LORD had said to Abra[ha]m:
"Leave your country, your people
and your father's household
and go to the land I will show you." *(Genesis 12:1)*

By faith Abraham, when he was called,
obeyed . . . and he went out,
not knowing where he was going. *(Hebrews 11:8, NASB)*

(ABRAHAM enters slowly, stops center stage; glances heavenward, looks out over audience, then back over his shoulder, heavenward again.)

ABRAHAM: Out there? *(He points toward rear of auditorium; nods; sighs)*
Out there!

(Addresses audience for the remainder of the monologue)

Beautiful country, out there. More beautiful, perhaps, than where we are right now. There is only one problem: That is out there—and my feet are planted right here.

Let me give you a simple lesson in geography. You know how the sun rises in the east *(points)* and sets in the west *(points)* and by knowing that, a person can determine not only east and west, but north and south as well? Well, forget it. Here is all you need to know about geography *(points toward his feet)*: Here—is familiar ground. *(Points toward rear of auditorium)* Out there—is unfamiliar country.

Let me give you a simple tip about traveling. You know how at night the front of the Big Dipper points you toward the North Star, by which you are able not only to find your way but also to know, more or less, which end is up? Well, forget about all that. The only thing you need to know about traveling is this *(points toward his feet)*: Here—is home, out there—is not home. *(Pause)*

Finally, let me share with you some simple advice about following God. You know all that stuff I just told you about here is home, here is familiar ground? Well, forget it. All you need to know about following God is this *(points toward his feet)*: Here is where I am. Out there—is where God wants me to be.

Simple, eh? So why am I so afraid to put one foot in front of the other and go?

Because—out there, is the future. *(Points)* And the future, by definition, is unknown. If it were already known, it would be known as the past. And the past is easy—well, not always easy but, good or bad, at least it holds no surprises, eh?

The future, on the other hand, holds nothing *but* surprises. Surprises—and the promises of God.

So what am I afraid of—that God will not honor His promises? That He will let me down? No—no. In my mind and in my heart I am full of faith.

(Beat, looks down)

But my feet, they are reluctant because—because—

(Quieter, gazing toward back of auditorium)

Because out there—possibly there will be unpleasantness, probably there will be problems, and certainly, there will be uncertainty—

(After a bit)

But you will excuse me, for I must go. For however frightening the future, I am a follower of God, and the feet of a follower of God—by definition, move only forward.

(Nods toward back of room)

Out there.

(After a moment, he begins to exit down center aisle as lights fade out.)

For Bitter or for Worse

Theme

Bitterness, anger, resentment

Scriptural Background

Hebrews 12:15

Tone

Slightly wacky

Cast

CORONER: *male or female*
SUPERVISOR: *male or female*
CORPSE: *male, preferably alive*

Scene

A morgue. A gurney on an empty stage will do.

Props

One gurney
Bag of potato chips
Ugly toy animal
Roots or branches
One lemon
Strand of film

Costumes

The CORONER wears a white lab coat.

SUPERVISOR may do the same or appear in a suit.

CORPSE is wearing a hospital gown or other simple clothing, the main function of which is to facilitate hiding the accessories on his body. These include a bag of potato chips attached to one shoulder and a "grudge" attached to the other (the latter looking remarkably like a stuffed toy animal, the uglier the better). There is also a bulge in the middle of his chest with perhaps a few roots or branches protruding (the bulge is a lemon beneath his shirt; this will be extracted during the CORONER's examination).

Summary

We are live at an autopsy. When the confused CORONER leaves the room, the CORPSE admits to the audience his *own* confusion as to why he's not as active as he used to be. The CORONER returns with his or her SUPERVISOR, who discovers the true cause of death: a bitter heart.

(From the opening we are live at an autopsy. CORPSE lies on gurney—dead, of course. Behind the gurney stands the CORONER, looking down at CORPSE in confusion. Finally, he or she throws up hands in frustration and begins to exit.)

CORONER *(calling offstage):* Dr. Jones! *Dr. Jones!*

(CORONER exits. After a few seconds, CORPSE turns his head toward audience, suddenly opens his eyes, then stiffly sits up. He looks both ways before addressing audience.)

CORPSE: I really shouldn't be sitting up like this—since I'm dead, but what's anybody gonna *do* about it since *(shrugs)* I'm dead! Besides, the doctor performing my autopsy stepped out for a minute. I think he [she] went to get his [her] supervisor—seems he's [she's] a bit confused about the cause of death. *(Stands)* Actually this death thing took me kinda by surprise. I mean, I'm in pretty good shape—I jog three or four times a week—or *used* to jog, you know what I mean. I tried to eat right, didn't overwork, had plenty of fun and relaxation, went to church on Sunday. I did pretty well in my Christian walk, too, if I say so myself. So I guess *I'm* kinda confused about the cause of death too. *(Hears something)* Here he [she] comes again. Shhh!

(Lies down, but in opposite direction as before. Realizes his mistake after a second or two, shoots look of consternation at audience, then sits up and lies down facing other direction as CORONER enters with SUPERVISOR. They stand behind CORPSE, facing audience.)

CORONER: I really appreciate you taking a look at this, sir [ma'am]. I've never seen anything quite like it. The most obvious thing is the ugly deformity on his left shoulder, but if you look closely you'll notice an unnatural growth on the other shoulder as well. (CORONER *turns* CORPSE's *face toward audience so doctors can gaze into top ear.*) And here in the brain is something they never told me about in medical school. But the thing that's really got me stumped is this *tree* stump right over his heart! I mean, I've heard of hardening of the arteries, but *this* guy's got a petrified *forest* growing in his chest!

(*Eyes of the* CORPSE *pop open; he blinks several times in astonishment before his head is rudely returned to faceup position by* CORONER.)

SUPERVISOR: Well, we're in luck—I've seen this disease before.

CORONER: You have?

SUPERVISOR: Yes. This tree stump, as you call it, is just the tip of the iceberg. Underneath is a system of roots that have bored deep into the man's heart.

CORONER: Amazing! What do you call it?

SUPERVISOR: The "Root of Bitterness." (*Turns face of* CORPSE *toward audience again so that he can pretend to pull film out of top ear*) It starts here, actually, in the mind. All of us make a permanent mental recording of the events of our lives—both good and bad.

(*He pulls from the ear of the* CORPSE *a long strand of film and hands it to the* CORONER, *who holds it up to the light, viewing in wide-eyed amazement scenes from the life of the* CORPSE. *This can be played up for as many laughs as possible, with the* CORONER *making faces, reacting with shock, looking scornfully at the* CORPSE, *and so forth. Finally,* CORONER *tosses it aside.*)

SUPERVISOR: The problem comes when people choose to replay the *bad* recordings, over and over again. Instead of employing confrontation and forgiveness when they feel they've been wronged, they allow their grievances to fester and grow until they've cultivated a full-grown root of bitterness, the fruit of which—(SUPERVISOR *reaches into the man's shirt and now struggles as though trying to free something that is tangled in the roots.* CORPSE *reacts appropriately, making anguished faces at the audience. Finally* SUPERVISOR *pulls out a big yellow lemon and holds it up for all to see.*)—is a bitter heart. It sours a person's personality and colors his perception, affecting his entire existence and everyone he comes in contact with. (*Tosses lemon behind him;* CORPSE *passes out.*)

CORONER: It sounds almost elementary when you explain it like that. But what about the strange growths on his shoulders?

SUPERVISOR: Ah yes. Those are pretty simple, too, once you've uncovered the root problem. People who keep a record of grievances and harbor bitterness in their hearts often have a chip on their shoulder.

(Amazed, CORONER removes bag of chips, examines then opens it, begins eating some.)

CORONER: *Mmmm.* Tasty. *(Eyes of CORPSE fly open in horror.)*

SUPERVISOR: As for the other shoulder, well, you'll almost inevitably find such people carrying: a grudge. *(CORPSE grimaces as SUPERVISOR dislodges ugly creature from his shoulder and holds it up.)* Sometimes for many years. Looks like he's been carrying *this* one around for a long time. Perhaps something his wife said to him 15 years ago—or something his folks did while he was a teenager. Or a pastor at a church he once attended—the possibilities are almost endless. The *results,* on the other hand, are quite predictable: the only conclusion we can draw about *this* fella is that the cause of death was irrelevant—he was already dead while he was still living!

(Begins covering body with a sheet. Shocked at this assessment, CORPSE looks wide-eyed and open-mouthed at audience one last time before sheet covers his face. CORONER and SUPERVISOR wheel gurney offstage. Perhaps the CORPSE squirms a bit beneath the sheet as gurney disappears through doorway or as lights go out.)

Achilles, Heal

Theme

Peter's denial of Christ; forgiving ourselves; realizing Christ's forgiveness

Tone

Serious with humor

Cast

PETER: *the apostle*

ABIGAIL: *a follower of Christ*

SHEVA: *a brassy, bombastic busybody; she runs the world in her spare time*

SHOBAL: *a buffoon*

TEMAN: *his fellow buffoon*

OFFICER: *a Temple guard, present in Gethsemane at the arrest of Jesus; unsympathetic toward Peter*

MAID: *a servant in the house of Chief Priest Caiaphas; a quiet girl, curious about Jesus*

TIRHANAH: *a young woman, servant to Caiaphas*

JESUS: *makes silent appearance at end*

GUARD: *makes silent appearance at end*

Scene

The courtyard of Chief Priest Caiaphas. An empty stage will do.

Props

A sack of coal (can be mimed)

Costumes

Clothing worn at the time of Christ. If done as a readers theatre, clothing may be uniform, perhaps black.

Production Notes

This play can be done effectively as a readers theater, without costumes or set and with minimal stage movement. Or it can be done as a regular drama. Or it can be done somewhere in between, perhaps with costumes and simple stage movement, but still as a readers theatre.

Regardless of format, the suggested order of the cast onstage is as follows: On the far left (stage right), up higher than the others, TIRHANAH. (Even in the readers theatre format, she should probably enter and exit as indicated in the script.)

A few feet to her left is SHEVA, then SHOBAL, TEMAN, OFFICER, MAID, PETER, ABIGAIL. ABIGAIL and PETER should be separated a bit from the others, and slightly forward. ABIGAIL and SHEVA should wait until their initial lines to enter, although if given as a readers theatre, this is not as important.

If done as a readers theatre it is not necessary for Jesus to appear, for it is through PETER (and through ABIGAIL) that the audience is invited to see Jesus in this play.

Summary

ABIGAIL comes upon the apostle PETER weeping. As he explains what happened in the courtyard during the trial of Jesus, the fateful scene around the fire unfolds in flashback. Later, ABIGAIL's true identity is revealed and she is able to encourage PETER with hope in Christ's readiness to forgive.

A Word About Achilles

(For program or bulletin; may be read aloud prior to play) In Greek mythology, Achilles was a virtually invincible warrior, but for a vulnerable spot in his heel. He was killed when an arrow, guided by the god Apollo, struck him in that very spot. Today, to mention someone's Achilles' heel is to refer to his or her weak spot, the point of vulnerability that leads to an eventual downfall.

For the apostle Peter, a would-be warrior for Jesus Christ, that downfall came in the heat of conflict when he ingloriously defended himself instead of the one for whom he had intended to lay down his life. His Achilles' heel was self-preservation.

There is no cure for injuries such as Peter suffered except to hear words of healing and forgiveness from the person against whom one has sinned. And so it is with our woeful warrior; his greatest need is to hear from the Captain of his heart the words: *Achilles, heal.*

(The scene begins somewhere in the darkness with PETER *onstage.* ABIGAIL *enters, searching. Her conversation with* PETER *will take them, via flashback, to the courtyard of Chief Priest Caiaphas, which may be represented merely by the actors in a semicircle around an imaginary fire, or in modest to extravagant detail.)*

ABIGAIL: Peter? *(No response)* Peter? *(Nothing)* I know you're there.

PETER *(dismal):* Who is it?

ABIGAIL: Abigail.

PETER: Always I welcome your company. But not tonight. Not now.

ABIGAIL: We were waiting outside the courtyard: Salome and Rachel and some of the others. We heard about Gethsemane and came as quickly as we could. I saw you running from the gate—I couldn't help but follow.

PETER *(on edge):* You heard me crying?

ABIGAIL: I—yes—it doesn't matter. I understand.

PETER: You sat there in the darkness and watched me weep?

ABIGAIL: I didn't watch you—no. *(Lower)* I couldn't help but overhear.

PETER *(angry):* Please leave me. Now.

ABIGAIL: If you drench the world around me with your tears, I have no choice but to dry them on my shoulder or else walk on soggy soil.

PETER: It is my own private flood. Please leave.

ABIGAIL: They wouldn't allow us in the courtyard! We have *no idea* what's happening! What are they doing to Him?

PETER *(numb):* Arranging His demise.

ABIGAIL: What?

PETER *(sarcastic):* The ecclesiastical council has kindly counted hands: All in favor say, "Die."

ABIGAIL: For what *reason?*

PETER: Blasphemy.

ABIGAIL: Blasphemy!

PETER *(angry):* Or for facing east instead of west! It doesn't matter. They wanted Him out of the picture, so they conveniently framed Him.

ABIGAIL: Then we must fight for Him.

PETER *(disillusioned):* Put down your sword.

ABIGAIL: I *have* no sword.

PETER: Then put down your good intentions. He prefers death.

ABIGAIL: He said so?

PETER: He would not let me fight for Him. *(Reflecting)* Or even, thinking back a bit, to fight rhetoric'ly against His dying.

ABIGAIL *(digesting this)*: And so you wept. You *love* Him. Why are you ashamed to weep for Him?

PETER: I do not weep . . . for Him.

ABIGAIL: Then why?

PETER *(wearily)*: We were . . . praying with Him in the garden when a crowd approached: Temple police, officers, servants of the Sanhedrin. You heard about Iscariot?

ABIGAIL: We heard.

PETER: And the arrest?

ABIGAIL: Everything up to the courtyard.

PETER: They took Him to Annas and then to the high priest. John and I were allowed through the gate because he's acquainted with Caiaphas. *(Lights come up on courtyard scene)* There was a fire in the center of the yard surrounded by servants and guards and a pair of buffoons. I joined the circle, ostensibly to warm myself but with the underlying intention of hearing whatever report might filter out to the crowd from inside the building.

(He has turned away from ABIGAIL *to join the others.* ABIGAIL *listens to the scene unfold but of course is not actually present, as* PETER *is.* SHEVA *enters from opposite side of stage.)*

SHOBAL: Hey, Sheva! Didja hear the news?

SHEVA: All I can hear is commotion. *What* news? And what are all these guards doing here? Are we at war? And if so, are we winning?

SHOBAL: They caught the Fisherman.

SHEVA: Fish get caught and fishermen do the catching. What in the world are you talking about?

SHOBAL: The *Fisherman.*

SHEVA: The *Galilean?*

SHOBAL: Pulled 'im in just a while ago.

TEMAN: Caught in the ol' net.

SHOBAL: Ain't gonna throw *this* one back.

SHEVA: So where is He?

TEMAN: They're grilling Him inside.

SHEVA: In there? *(Jerks a thumb toward the porch)*

SHOBAL: Sure as the devil's in hell.

SHEVA: If the devil were in hell, we'd all rest easy. Go study your theology. So they've finally sunk to sinking their teeth in the Galilean, huh?

TEMAN: Picked 'im up in Gethsemane. Me and Shobal were part o' the posse. (SHOBAL *grins with pride.*)

SHEVA: And he's in there with ol' Pieface?

SHOBAL *(wary):* I wouldn't refer to Caiaphas that way while standing outside his house, if I were you.

SHEVA: Well, you're not me and I've called him worse than that to his face. So shut up and tell me what's happening here. Are they alone?

(SHOBAL *is confused: should he shut up or reply?*)

MAID: Them and the Seventy.

SHEVA: The Sanhedrin?

MAID: Yes, ma'am. Tirhanah is up on the porch, listening through the window, keeping us informed.

TEMAN: Giving us the lowdown from way up high.

SHOBAL: The lowdown from the high court.

MAID: Here she is now. What's the word, Tirhanah?

TIRHANAH *(enters):* More witnesses. And more confusion. One fellow swore on his grandmother's grave that the Galilean threatened to destroy the Temple. And then *another* fellow swore on the *Temple* that the Galilean threatened to destroy the grave belonging to the first fellow's *grandmother*! They can't agree on *anything!*

PETER *(cautiously):* And what—does the Galilean say?

(Subtly, the OFFICER *recognizes the voice.)*

TIRHANAH: Nothing.

SHEVA: Nothing?

TIRHANAH: Nothing. No alibis, rebuttal, or defense.

SHEVA: Hurry! Go back and tell us more of what He doesn't say. *(She exits.)*

OFFICER: He offered no resistance in Gethsemane as well. One of His followers, however, took it upon himself—

SHOBAL (*aware of what's coming*): Listen to this one, Sheva—

SHEVA: How can I, with you crowing in my ear?

OFFICER: As I was saying, one of his compatriots (*looks suspiciously at* PETER) . . . pulled out a sword and, clumsily—not unlike a man casting a net on the Sea of Galilee—assailed the skull of Malchus, one of the servants here in this house.

SHEVA (*concerned*): He cut Malchus down the middle?

OFFICER: Actually—

TEMA: Hey, here's one: Wha'd the guy say who got his head sliced in two?

SHOBAL: I don' know—wha'd he say?

TEMAN: I've got half a mind to make you pay for this!

SHOBAL (*giggling*): No—no—he says—he says—I'm trying very hard to be open-minded about this!

SHEVA: And I'm trying very hard not to filet your faces! How's *that* for being open-minded?

SHOBAL (*suddenly serious*): That's good. That's good.

TEMAN (*likewise*): Very good.

SHEVA: Now, could we please hear the rest of the story?

OFFICER: There *is* none. Except that he leaned to the left and lost an earring and his hearing on the right.

SHOBAL (*to* TEMAN): Ear today, gone tomorrow. (TEMAN *grins.*)

MAID: Malchus is fine. I saw him inside with both of his ears intact and telling a tale with his tongue of a miracle: Jesus made him whole.

TEMAN: Happy new ear!

SHEVA (*flabbergasted*): He grew back his ear?

MAID: Got back the old one.

SHEVA: A likely story.

SHOBAL (*a riddle*): Hey—wha'd the guy say when he put the man's ear back on?

TEMAN: I don' know—wha'd he say?

SHOBAL: Ears *to* yah!

SHEVA (*to* TEMAN *and* SHOBAL; *exasperated*): Would to God that the man with the sword were here in this court to remove your tongues by decapitation! (*To* OFFICER) Are you telling me that the Fisherman somehow replaced an ear that had been defaced?

OFFICER: I saw only the removal. I did not see the repair. It was black as midnight.

SHOBAL: It *was* midnight.

SHEVA: Suppose there was enough absence of light for a fake physician to perform some crafty sleight-of-hand on a slightly damaged ear—the dabbing of blood, rearrangement of hair—then brag that he'd managed a miracle, hoping to impress the arresting officers into setting Him free. He's said to be a powerful speaker. Perhaps He's a fast talker as well.

PETER (*his loyalty to the truth getting the best of him*): He *heals* people. (*They turn to look at him.*) At least, that's what I heard.

(*He turns away, uneasy.* OFFICER, MAID, *and* SHEVA *continue watching him, increasingly suspicious.*)

TEMAN (*privately*): Hey, Shobal—know what *I* heard?

SHOBAL: What?

TEMAN: Sheep. (*No response*) Get it? I herd: sheep.

SHOBAL: That's not even funny. (*After a moment*) Hey, Sheva—

SHEVA: Yeah? (*Her eyes never leave* PETER.)

SHOBAL: Know what *I* heard?

SHEVA: No—wha' did you hear?

SHOBAL (*thinks about it, realizes it won't work*): Never mind.

SHEVA (*ignoring him*): You, there—gazing at Ursa Major as though the constellations counted for something.

PETER: Me?

SHEVA: No—Pontius Pilate. Yes, you. Why are you here?

PETER: On earth?

SHEVA: Fool. In this courtyard, warming yourself by this flimsy fire.

PETER (*searching for words*): I—came with a friend. He's around here—somewhere. We were passing by and we heard the upheaval.

OFFICER: Then you weren't in the garden?

PETER: Gethsemane? No, never. (*Beat*) Not recently. Not tonight. (*Looks away, trying to act casual. All eyes on him.*)

SHEVA *(plotting):* Officer, in the garden this evening, regarding Malchus and the magic ear—did they catch the klutz who did the cutting?

OFFICER *(staring at* PETER*):* No. His followers followed their hearts and raced away. It would have made no difference, though—the evidence *(taps his ear)* has been tampered with.

SHEVA: Don't waste your breath splitting hairs about evidence. It's enough for Caiaphas that his right-hand man had to take it on the chin. There's no turning the other cheek with the high priest: An eye for an eye and a tooth for a tooth is the rule of thumb in *this* neck of the woods. Caiaphas would make that man pay through the nose for taking arms against an ear.

OFFICER: I'd love to see his head upon a platter, but nobody saw his face in the dark. We've only his Galilean tongue to tell him by, and the man would be risking life and limb to show his voice around *here* again soon.

SHEVA *(up to something; to* PETER*):* Sir, this fire has lost it's will to live. Do us a cozy favor and hand me that sack of fuel chips there.

PETER *(seeing sack behind him):* This?

SHEVA: Yes. It's full of those thingamajigs—I always forget what they're called.

PETER: Briquettes. *(Leans over to pick up sack)*

SHEVA, OFFICER, SHOBAL, TEMAN: Wrong. (PETER *freezes.)*

SHEVA: In Galilee, maybe. Down here, south of Samaria, we call it coal. You're one of His gang.

PETER: OK, I admit it: I grew up in Galilee. That doesn't mean I know the man from Nazareth. Just because I was born in His vicinity, does that prove that I'm a friend of His?

SHEVA *(solemn):* I don't know. Time will tell.

TEMAN *(derisive):* Hey, Shobal—how many Galileans does it take to clean a dozen fish?

SHOBAL: I don't know. How many Galileans *does* it take to clean a dozen fish?

TEMAN: Twenty-four. Twelve to hold the fish and 12 more to hold the fish's noses.

(Laughing, he and SHOBAL *plug their own noses.)*

TIRHANAH *(entering):* Fire! Fire! Fire in the council chambers!

SHEVA: The house is made of sand. It's noncombustible.

TIRHANAH: I know. But tempers are flaring, blood is boiling, and bigwigs are burning with indignation!

SHOBAL (*enthusiastic*): I *love* a good housewarming.

SHEVA (*sarcastic*): Hmm, wha' d'ya suppose ignited them?

TEMA: An inflammatory remark?

TIRHANAH: Temperatures were already rising, in light of the prisoner's propensity for silence in the face of convoluted questioning, so Caiaphas, incensed, put it to Him straight: Are you the Messiah, the Son of God?

SHOBAL: Now there's a question you don't hear every day.

MAID: And how did the victim reply?

TIRHANAH: You won't *believe* what He said.

SHEVA: Try us.

TIRHANAH: He said He *was.*

SHEVA: You're right. We don't believe it.

MAID: Speak for yourself. *I'd* be willing to consider it true. Did He offer any proof?

TIRHANAH (*sweeping a hand across heaven*): He said there would come a day when they would see Him riding a cumulonimbus caravan across the sky.

SHOBAL: That would do it for *me.*

OFFICER: Yeah, well, Caiaphas'll bring 'im back down to earth.

TIRHANAH: He did the next best thing—

TEMAN: Went through the roof?

TIRHANAH: No. Red in the face and hot under the collar, the high priest tore his robe, letting off steam.

SHOBAL: More mending for the maid.

TIRHANAH: Then he blared out: Blasphemy! And called for a ballot.

SHEVA: The result of which—

TIRHANAH: I don't know. I came out to fill you in.

SHEVA: The outcome is inescapable—He's dug himself a pit. By now they'll be passing sentence. Quick! Go bring us the rest of the paragraph.

(TIRHANAH *exits.* TEMAN *and* SHOBAL *turn and face the house to engage in the following conversation. It is a private dialogue; they pay no attention to the* MAID's *lines. Nor does she hear their comments, caught up as she is in a hopeful recitation of reports she has heard.*)

TEMAN (*to* SHOBAL): He's in pretty deep, that's fer sure.

MAID (*to* PETER): Is it true what they say about Him?

PETER (*turning away from her):* How would *I* know?

SHOBAL (*to* TEMAN): Yeah—up to His neck this time, I'm afraid.

MAID: They say that He could calm the storm!

TEMAN: Be a long time before *this* thing blows over.

MAID: They say that He could feed 5,000!

SHOBAL: Bit off more than He could chew.

MAID: They say that He could walk on water!

TEMAN: He's on thin ice *now,* let me tell ya.

MAID: They say that He could cure the deaf!

SHOBAL: Like t' hear 'im talk His way outta *this* one.

MAID: They say that He could cure the lame!

TEMAN: Walked right into it, what can ya say?

MAID: They say that He could cure the blind!

SHOBAL: Shoulda been able t' see it coming.

MAID: They say that He could cast out demons!

TEMAN: Who the devil does He think He is, anyway?

MAID: They say that He could raise the dead!

SHOBAL: Kills me how He got away with it for so long.

MAID: They say that He spoke of a second birth!

TEMAN: Some people are born to trouble, 's all *I* can say.

MAID: They say that He spoke of eternal life!

SHOBAL: Caiaphas will put an end to things, wait and see.

OFFICER: Here comes the woman back from the front—

TIRHANAH (*rushing in):* The council has pronounced the verdict!

SHEVA: And what have they mumbled this time?

TIRHANAH: Their diction was flawless: Guilty as charged.

PETER (*stunned):* Guilty? (MAID *is staring at him intently.)*

TIRHANAH: Unanimous. All for one and one for all.

MAID (*admiringly*): You're one of them, aren't you.

(*Her following comments are to* PETER, *his are to her, and* TIRHANAH's *are to anyone who has ears to hear. The lines are spoken quickly and almost on top of each other.*)

PETER: *What?*

TIRHANAH: You should have seen it—

MAID: I recognize you now—

PETER: I don't think so—

TIRHANAH: It was a madhouse!

MAID: I knew you looked familiar—

PETER: You must be mistaken—

TIRHANAH: A riot!

MAID: But I couldn't put my finger on it.

PETER: Go tend to your duties!

TIRHANAH: A free-for-all! Except for the prisoner, of course.

MAID: Now I remember where I've *seen* you before!

PETER: Just leave me alone!

TIRHANAH: Anarchy was the rule of the day!

MAID: You were with Him at the Temple—

PETER: You're crazy—I'm not even religious!

TIRHANAH: Fists were high and blows were low!

MAID: They brought out a woman caught in the act—

PETER: What are you talking about?

TIRHANAH: They hurled insults at Him—

MAID: They wanted to stone her—

PETER: I don't remember!

TIRHANAH: They covered His eyes—

MAID: They asked His opinion: What shall we do?

TIRHANAH: And then they hit Him!

MAID: Moses says stone her: What say You?

TIRHANAH: They said: Prophesy, Preacher! Who's punching You now?

MAID: Your leader knelt down and drew in the dust—

PETER: He's not my leader, so shut your mouth!

TIRHANAH: They all agreed that Jesus must die.

MAID: I cannot read, so I read your lips—

TIRHANAH: They want Him dead, but they don't have the right—

MAID: You whispered the words that He wrote on the ground?

TIRHANAH: So they're taking Him off to a Roman court!

MAID (*spreads her hands, indicating ground*): "All who are born are guilty of sin."

TIRHANAH: Here they come now! Look—there He is!

(*All but* PETER *turn to look in the direction* TIRHANAH *is pointing. Jesus has been led by a guard to the top of the porch.* PETER *shouts at the top of his lungs.*)

PETER: *I never met Him, so help me God!*

(*The intensity of the dramatic moment will require a substantial pause.* TIRHANAH *looks at Jesus, who is staring lovingly at* PETER.)

TIRHANAH: Why does He stare at that man over there?

(*Her innocent question is delivered in marked contrast to the crescendo that leads up to it. As* PETER *slowly turns his head to look at Jesus, all other heads turn to look at the disciple. The cast freezes in this position as the* MAID *makes her final statement.*)

MAID (*sweetly*): See? He *knows* you. He recognized your voice.

(*Her words cause* PETER *to bury his face in his hands as the lights fade out on all but him and* ABIGAIL. *When* ABIGAIL *finally speaks, it is with compassion and tenderness.*)

ABIGAIL: And that is when you ran.

PETER: They didn't even follow—

ABIGAIL: Some did. But their captain called them off.

PETER: I wish he hadn't. It would have been less painful. (*Gathering his grief*) What a belching, bleating, imbecilic fool am I to call myself a rescuer of His! I am a hero only of hypocrisy!

ABIGAIL: Do not assume that a moment of weakness nullifies the moments of nobility.

PETER: That is exactly my assumption.

ABIGAIL: Just because a man has a weak ankle, does it therefore follow—

PETER *(interrupting):* Weak knees, Abigail. Let your analogy reflect the truth: weak knees.

ABIGAIL *(persisting):* Just because a man has a weak ankle, does it mean there is no strength in his entire frame? You are merely a man with a limp in a race of limpers.

PETER: And I am losing that race.

ABIGAIL: It was . . . the human race to which I was referring.

PETER: There are those who limp and those who crawl.

ABIGAIL *(upbeat):* You will walk again with dignity.

PETER *(exploding):* You don't understand! They will kill Him! he predicted it, but we were as deaf to His prediction. As a man without ears! *(Calmer now, confessing)* I told you we prayed with Him in the garden—*He* spread His life upon a rock imploring heaven for reprieve, while we in the background, gathering strength for our escape, accompanied His solitary requiem with the dissonant dirge of our sinuses!

ABIGAIL: Speak plainly, Peter.

PETER *(roaring):* We snored! Is that plainly enough for you? *(Lamenting)* We snored—and I the loudest.

ABIGAIL *(unsure of what to say):* You were tired. Next time you will do better—

PETER: They are going to kill Him! And the last thing, the last memory He will have of me is that I, who said that I would die for Him, had not even the courage to call Him my friend.

ABIGAIL *(after a bit):* He is good at forgiveness.

PETER: It is forgiving myself that will take a lifetime.

ABIGAIL: I, too, have climbed that mountain.

PETER: You?

ABIGAIL: Have you forgotten where you found me, you and your leader?

PETER *(it comes to him):* Yes. I *had* forgotten. *(Recalling)* "Go and sin no more," He said.

ABIGAIL: "Woman, where are thine accusers? Hath no one condemned thee?"

PETER: "No one, Lord," said you.

ABIGAIL: "Then neither do I condemn thee," said He. "Neither do I . . . condemn thee . . ."

PETER: Perhaps . . . He would somehow . . . understand.

ABIGAIL *(looks at him):* Perhaps He loves you . . . just a bit.

(PETER *turns and looks at her with big, sad, hopeful eyes as the lights slowly fade out.)*

All the King's Horses and All the King's Men

Theme

Child sexual abuse

Tone

Very serious

Cast

WOMAN: *in her mid-30s or older; feeling betrayed*
PASTOR: *50 or older; caught in a difficult situation*

Scene

The sanctuary of a church. A pew or two, or a row of chairs.

Costumes

Modern

Summary

A woman returns to the scene of her father's recent funeral where she angrily confronts the pastor who so eloquently eulogized the man who robbed her of her innocence.

(At rise, a woman enters and sits in a chair or pew. After a short time of inner struggle she rises, sits, rises again, as though wishing to speak. While she is doing this, PASTOR has entered casually behind her, on his way somewhere. He stops when he sees her, observes and listens, curious. The WOMAN rises a third time, having apparently found the courage to speak; in fact, she shouts.)

WOMAN: Stop it—! Stop it! What you're doing is wrong—! What you're saying—It's wrong—it's all—He wasn't like that—It's not true!

(WOMAN sits, slumps over in the pew. The PASTOR approaches tentatively, speaks gently.)

PASTOR: What isn't true? *(WOMAN leaps to her feet, spins, staring at him as he continues . . .)* I'm sorry—I was passing through the church on the way to my office. I'm Pastor Frasier. Carl—Frasier. I saw you standing, you seemed . . . upset. I thought perhaps—*(She is verbose in her silence.)* Can I *help* you? *(There is no response.)* You look vaguely familiar, I—Do I know you? Have we met? I'm sorry, you've probably been attending here for some time and I'm not recognizing you. The church has gotten so large in the past few years, I don't always know my own congregation very well.

WOMAN: That's the first thing I've heard you say that even remotely resembles the truth.

PASTOR: So you've heard me preach. *(Realizes what he's just said)* Now there's a self-incriminating statement if I've ever heard one! *(He laughs, she does not.)* What I mean is—it sounds like you've developed an opinion. About my preaching. Apparently you've been attending here.

WOMAN: I was referring to your knowledge of the congregation you supposedly serve.

PASTOR: Well, again, I apologize. As I said, it's difficult to keep up with all the new—

WOMAN *(interrupting):* My parents have attended your church since my father's retirement several years ago.

PASTOR: And you have heard them express some . . . dissatisfaction?

WOMAN: They've never said anything one way or the other.

PASTOR: Well, no news is good news, I suppose.

WOMAN: My parents have not spoken to me for six and a half years.

PASTOR: Oh. I see.

WOMAN: I doubt very much that you do. *(Now it is the PASTOR's turn to respond with silence.)* My father will never speak to me again. You buried him last Thursday.

PASTOR: You must be Clarissa.

WOMAN: I must be.

PASTOR: I looked for you at the funeral, with the family—

WOMAN: I didn't sit with my family. I sat here, in the back.

(He doesn't know what to say, but he speaks anyway.)

PASTOR: It was a large turnout. He had . . . many friends here. A fine man. Well liked. Of course I realize that things were—

(She tilts her head, challenging him.)

WOMAN: How *were* things?

(Aware of the challenge, he struggles onward.)

PASTOR: He spoke of you . . . on several occasions.

WOMAN: Then he actually remembered me.

PASTOR: Not in detail, of course.

WOMAN: No, he wouldn't have wanted to get into specifics.

PASTOR: But he spoke of you with a certain degree of . . . of sadness and disappointment. Not in *you*, of course, but disappointment that something, that something had come between you.

WOMAN: Between us.

PASTOR: Yes, he never said exactly what it was, but—

WOMAN: Something had come between us, is that how he put it? *(She is amused, in a bitter sort of way.)* Something had come between us?

PASTOR: I think, yes, more or less, that's how he described it.

WOMAN: How incredibly civilized of him.

PASTOR *(unsure how to continue)*: He always spoke of you with fondness.

WOMAN *(betraying no warmth)*: He loved me very much.

PASTOR: It's . . . good that you can feel that way.

WOMAN: And often.

PASTOR: Pardon?

WOMAN: I said my father loved me very much. And very often.

(PASTOR's throat tightens slightly, his chin rises.)

PASTOR: I'm afraid I don't understand.

WOMAN: Interesting. Exactly my thoughts as a five-year-old concubine: I was afraid, and I didn't understand.

(He is not so much bailing out as he is realizing that he's in over his head.)

PASTOR: Perhaps you would like to schedule an appointment with my secretary. I do counseling on Tuesdays and every other—

WOMAN *(interrupting):* I came back here today to speak my mind.

PASTOR: To me?

WOMAN: To the walls. I thought the place was empty.

(PASTOR turns, indicating the direction of his office.)

PASTOR: I had to come back. I'd forgotten my notes for tonight's—

WOMAN *(interrupting):* What you forgot was the truth.

PASTOR: Twice now you've made reference to my lack of truthfulness, but I'm not sure—

WOMAN: I came back here today to say to the walls, to the pews, to the stinking cockroaches if they have ears and have the time to listen, what I couldn't say last Thursday at the funeral, what I should have stood up and shouted in front of the entire congregation as they . . . as they listened to you eulogize and idolize and practically *canonize* the criminal who stole everything in life from me that really mattered!

PASTOR *(trying to hold his ground):* And what was it you would have shouted?

WOMAN: That it wasn't true, that golden calf you created from the pulpit last Thursday.

(His retreat is imminent, but for now he speaks carefully.)

PASTOR: But it *was* true, as far as it went, as far as I knew. Regardless of an individual's . . . private flaws and imperfections, it is important to the survivors to mark his passing in as positive a light as possible. And I *do* have a high regard for your father, as a friend and as a scholar.

WOMAN: Yes, I remember. The plaque.

PASTOR: I beg your pardon?

WOMAN: You said that you were planning to put up a plaque on the wall of the church library in his memory.

PASTOR: Your father was always very helpful to me in my sermon preparation. I—trusted him with—matters of importance. He seemed to love nothing better than spending quiet hours in the library, doing theological research.

WOMAN: Strange how a man's hobbies change with the passage of time, isn't it?

(The sarcasm in her voice cannot quite cover the lump in her throat.)

PASTOR: I'm just saying that there was a side to him that was very—

WOMAN *(interrupting):* No, keep the plaque idea. And perhaps the youth group could donate books on child sexual abuse and inscribe inside the covers: In memory of Jason Richardson, who loved children.

(A brief period of time elapses.)

PASTOR: I knew that there were problems in your family—

(She turns on him, suddenly, viciously.)

WOMAN: There were no "problems" in my family. There was a man who was incredibly confused about the right and proper use of his sexuality.

(In his discomfort, he retreats to the familiar.)

PASTOR: If you'd like to come into my office—

WOMAN: I do not go behind closed doors with men.

PASTOR: I understand. *(Stumbles for words)* What I'm wondering, for your own peace of mind—whether it seems like a person deserves it or not, often we find in the church, or outside it, for that matter, that if a person is able to come to terms with the offense, if he or she is able to—

WOMAN: I know what forgiveness is. I just don't know what it is in relation to this kind of violation.

PASTOR: I'm not pretending it's an easy thing to do.

WOMAN: I'm not pretending I haven't tried. *(She has come this far; she may as well finish.)* One afternoon when I was almost 17, a junior in high school, I excused myself from study hall, caught a bus downtown and gathering up all of the courage a kid can accumulate through a dozen years of hell, I walked through the front door of the police station to report my father to the authorities. We lived in a fairly small town, so the entrance to the station was located in the lobby of city hall, and on that particular afternoon there were several older men sitting on benches across the lobby, apparently waiting for a meeting to begin. The officer on duty, a woman, sat behind a bulletproof window with a small speaker in the middle of it. I was crying when I entered and terribly afraid of what I was about to do and my words when I spoke them were not very loud. "I wish to report my father for sexual abuse," I said. The woman behind the window spoke with an amplified voice entirely devoid of compassion and said, "I can't hear you—would you please speak directly into the microphone?" and the men across the lobby looked up from their conversation and stared at me and when I looked back at them, struggling for the strength to repeat what I had just said, I discovered that as they sat there on their benches gazing curiously in my direction, they bore a remarkable resemblance to a church full of hypocrites sitting in their cozy little pews and I was reminded of my father's doting and devoted congregation and I realized in that excruciating moment, that no one in the world—or at least in my little nearsighted section of it—would ever in a thousand years be willing to take my side. Besides, I'd already said it once and it seemed like there could not possibly be anything more difficult than to say again the words that I'd just said, to annunciate my most private shame through a microphone in a window in front of an audience of men, so I turned around and ran down the crumbling stone steps of city hall and back into the prison I called my home.

PASTOR: And never said anything?

WOMAN: Eventually. Friends here and there. A series of counselors. A former husband or two.

PASTOR: And now me.

WOMAN: The consequences of eavesdropping.

PASTOR: You said yourself that you came back here to say what you could not say at the funeral. In your heart you were wishing you could tell me—and now you have. (WOMAN *nods*.) I wonder if I may ask, what did you hope to accomplish today?

WOMAN (*looking up*): Accomplish?

PASTOR: Will it be enough for you—today's proclamation? Or had you spoken out at the funeral, would that have satisfied you?

WOMAN: The truth would be known.

PASTOR: Yes. But for yourself . . . for your future.

WOMAN: Are you suggesting that I have one?

PASTOR (*with confidence, warmth*): I am suggesting that with the help of God and the compassion of an understanding friend and given ample opportunity to grieve your losses, that healing—however remote it may seem from where you are now—that healing is possible.

(WOMAN *looks away, wanting to believe*.)

PASTOR: It will take time, of course.

WOMAN: Time is short. I only have one lifetime.

PASTOR (*gently, after a moment*): Then perhaps it is time to begin.

(WOMAN *slowly turns to look at* PASTOR. *Tears stream down her cheeks. Lights slowly fade to blackout*.)

Idle Idols: False Gods and Barbie Dolls

Theme

Twentieth-century idolatry; worship

Tone

Farcical

Cast

Newscaster: *male or female*

Dr. Louis Let's-Be-Sneaky: *male or female* (Lois), named after late British paleontologist Louis S. B. Leaky.

Scene

A television interview. A couple of chairs are sufficient.

Props

Golf club
Tennis racket
Barbie doll in gown
Small plastic basketball player statue
Popular magazines
TV Guide
Video game instruction manual
Key chain with four keys
Stereo headphones
Political convention hat

Political pennant or banner

Sports team pennant

Costumes

Futuristic (have fun!)

Summary

It is far in the future, and earth is little more than an ancient burial ground. Digging deep, an alien archaeologist uncovers artifacts that give him clues to the worship practices of 20th-century Americans. In light of the evidence, can it be ascertained that *God* was the object of our adoration?

(As sketch opens NEWSCASTER *and* DR. SNEAKY *are already in position, perhaps sitting, for a television interview.* NEWSCASTER *holds a microphone. All props are out of sight until needed.)*

NEWSCASTER: Good evening, and welcome to *Archaeology Update.* This is Tom Broke-jaw [or Lonnie Lung if female] for Channel 4,863. I'm coming to you live from City No. 27 on Planet No. 3 of Star No. 426 in Galaxy No. 837. On tonight's program we will be visiting with renowned archaeologist Louis Let's-Be-Sneaky. Good evening, Dr. Sneaky. (SNEAKY *nods, smiles.)* Dr. Sneaky has recently made an exciting discovery regarding the worship habits of 20th-century humans. He and his crew have just returned from an archaeology dig on Planet No. 1 of Star No. 1 in Galaxy No. 1. You may remember it from your history lessons as the planet once known as Earth, the dismal, dirty, garbage-laden planet where human beings originated. Of course, that was many centuries ago before the mass exodus into space during the cruel and ruthless 50-year world dictatorship of [insert name of someone your congregation will chuckle over]. Nowadays the planet is inhabited only by a few wandering tribes believed to be the descendants of the now-outlawed [insert name of your church or denomination]. Dr. Sneaky, how long did you and your crew have to dig before you uncovered the first relics of 20th-century religious worship?

DR. SNEAKY: About two-and-a-half weeks.

NEWSCASTER: Which by modern archaeological standards is quite a long time, what with the recent developments in excavation technology—am I correct?

DR. SNEAKY: A very long time. But of course we expected it to take at least that much time because, you see, anywhere one goes on Planet Earth one has to excavate through some 30 to 40 feet of garbage, because the whole planet, you see, is covered with the stuff. Except for the oceans, of course; they're covered with 40 feet of oil.

NEWSCASTER: So I understand. Now I presume, modern science being what it is, that you had some idea as to where to dig and what you would find when you'd done your digging.

DR. SNEAKY: Exactly. Our Search Computers—SC9000 for those of you who are interested in those things—predicted the exact location of what appeared to be an extensive collection of ancient artifacts in fairly good condition. Exactly what they would be we wouldn't know until we unearthed them, but we felt pretty sure we were on to something good.

NEWSCASTER: And as it turns out, "something good" is hardly an adequate description for what you've uncovered. News sources have been quoted as calling this the "greatest archaeological find in recent history," surpassing even the discovery 75 years ago of Elvis's footprints on Planet Spielberg. Tell us, Dr. Sneaky, what exactly have you found?

DR. SNEAKY: All of our preliminary calculations indicate that we have uncovered a 20th-century worship site, replete with prayer books, worship manuals, and a variety of idols.

NEWSCASTER: Doctor, there may be some in our viewing audience who are not familiar with so archaic a concept as an "idol," living as we do in a monotheistic society. Before you show us a few samples, explain to us, if you will, what exactly *is* an idol?

DR. SNEAKY: Certainly. Strange as it may sound, an idol is a statue or other sacred object that was given attention, affection, or adulation by humans. In short, they were their gods. Here is one of the more interesting ones we discovered. (*Holds up golf club*)

NEWSCASTER: They would actually bow down and worship this idol?

DR. SNEAKY: We're not sure, exactly. There appears to be some sort of a handle or grip at one end. We think perhaps they held it above their heads (*does so*) and carried it in parades in honor of the Tall-skinny-god-with-the-big-head. (*Lifts up tennis racket*) This one is very similar and may be just another conception of what essentially was the same god.

NEWSCASTER: God or goddess?

DR. SNEAKY: Well, we're not quite sure. Many of their idols appear to be asexual. (*Brings out Barbie doll*) This one, however, seems definitely to be a goddess.

NEWSCASTER: A fertility goddess?

DR. SNEAKY: Again, we're not entirely certain. We believe she may have represented the early humans' insatiable fascination with the female figure. But notice also that she is dressed in a rather beautiful gown.

NEWSCASTER: With matching shoes and handbag, no less—

DR. SNEAKY: Exactly. This leads us to suspect that this particular idol represented a goddess whose attributes exemplified both physical form *and* outward attire.

NEWSCASTER: Is it safe to argue that human beings in the 20th century may have been obsessed with both the body *beneath* the clothing and the need or desire to *hide* that body beneath the most exquisite of apparel?

DR. SNEAKY: Quite safe, quite safe. Now some of their gods were perceived as being more masculine in appearance. *(Lifts up plastic statue of basketball star)* This one, for instance, is the god M-Jordan. *(Or some other relevant star)*

NEWSCASTER: He appears to be holding a sphere of some sort in his hand. Is that supposed to be the Planet Earth?

DR. SNEAKY: Yes, I'm quite sure of it. Perhaps M-Jordan was perceived to be the god who caused the world to turn.

NEWSCASTER: I guess that would make him the one on whom the sun rises and sets, wouldn't it?

DR. SNEAKY: Something like that, yes. We believe this may have been the god for whom the song was written: "He's Got the Whole World in His Hands." *(Reaching for magazines)* We also uncovered what are almost certainly some sort of worship manuals and prayer books. For example, here's one—can you get a close-up shot? *(Holds it up)* A bit difficult to read, as you can see, but we can almost make out the title: How-to-something-something-Nintendo. Probably: How to Worship the God Nintendo—or words to that effect. And here's another. *(Holds up "TV Guide"; reads title)* Tee-Vee Guide. Some kind of guide to worship, no doubt. *(Opens and flips through pages)* Almost indecipherable inside except for the words: *As the World Turns*. Obviously another reference to the god M-Jordan.

NEWSCASTER: Perhaps part of a prayer.

DR. SNEAKY: Exactly. *(Takes out key chain)* And this, we believe, is a sort of prayer chain—similar to the prayer beads we've found in other archaic cultures. *(Displays keys)* Each flat metal device probably represents some sort of god, which they could worship while grasping that particular representative piece of metal. Sounds silly, I know, but remember, we're talking about the 20th century. Here's one, for instance, labeled Mercedes. And this one's marked BMW: We're not sure how to pronounce that word. Our linguists are working on it. Here's one marked Fla Condo. We don't know what Fla means either, but it's, again, obviously the name of one of their many gods. *(Reads)* Calif Condo. *(Shrugs)* And this one: Seabreeze III. As I said, many idols, many gods.

NEWSCASTER: It's no wonder their culture collapsed.

DR. SNEAKY: Exactly! No singular focus for their worship! Scattered adoration inevitably leads to scattered brains. History has proven that over and over again. I remember once on Planet Jerry-Garcia, how—

NEWSCASTER: Excuse me, Dr. Sneaky, but we're almost out of time.

DR. SNEAKY: Yes—well, then, perhaps I have just enough time to quickly show you just a few more fascinating artifacts. These were apparently some sort of headgear worn in worship by Earthlings.

(SNEAKY *has taken out stereo headphones and gives them to* NEWSCASTER, *who dons them incorrectly, creating a football face mask-effect across his mouth.* SNEAKY *puts political convention hat on his own head and has in his hands two pennants, one with a politician's name on it, which he will keep, and the other with a popular sports team's name on it, which he will give to* NEWSCASTER.)

And this, too, it seems, was some sort of ceremonial head covering for use in worship services. And these . . . flags, if you will, were probably waved as some sort of praise device before their gods and goddesses.

(*They wave their pennants and, with their empty hands, pick up and begin waving golf club and Barbie doll.*)

NEWSCASTER: I can see why they'd enjoy worshiping their idols—it's fun!

DR. SNEAKY: Exactly! We believe they would work themselves into a regular religious frenzy of adoration! Archaic, but awfully cute, don't you think?

NEWSCASTER (*as they exit, marching*): That's all the time we have. Good night, everybody!

(*Lights out*)

Persons Who Shall Remain Nameless

(History in the Making)

Theme

The abortion issue; consequences of our choices

Tone

Very serious

Cast

Speaking parts

DIRECTOR: *a woman of any age*

ASSISTANT: *a woman of any age*

ANONYMOUS: *a young woman*

MARIA VAN BEETHOVEN: *says one line*

JUSTYNA CHOPIN: *says one line*

TAISSA SOLZHENITSYN: *says one line*

ROSA BOJAXHIU: *says her name only*

Extras: Other women (29 or fewer). Note that the number of women's names on the list can vary based on availability of actors; the director may also want to add or subtract names according to need or preference.)

Scene

A waiting room: chairs, etc.

Props

Clipboard
Pen
Magazines

Costumes

Please see Production Notes.

Production Notes

There are several ways in which to present this script. You may wish for a stylistic interpretation, with dim lights, stark shadows, the women dressed in dark, austere clothing, for instance. Or you may go for a more realistic setting featuring a normal waiting room, normal lighting, modern costumes. A third choice would be to use period costumes (with each woman wearing the appropriate clothing for the time in which she lived) in either a modern or stylized setting.

Summary

Two dozen or so women sit in a waiting room at a large pregnancy termination facility. As their names are called, mothers of some of history's most influential men and women rise and exit toward off-stage operating rooms, where their would-be famous offspring cease to be.

(*At rise, a group of 20 to 29 women of childbearing age are sitting in the waiting room of a large clinic. Their mood is somber, with some of them perhaps reading or knitting, others chatting quietly or staring off into space. After a few moments, the* DIRECTOR *and her* ASSISTANT *enter.*)

DIRECTOR: Good morning, ladies. How is everybody today? (*She is met with a combination of blank stares, tiny nods, and a few polite smiles.*) Well, the sooner we begin, the sooner we'll be finished, I always say, so why don't I start with a brief introduction, and then we can get on with the procedure.

ANONYMOUS: Abortion.

DIRECTOR (*barely phased*): Yes, well, call it whatever you like, we're here to help you go through with a choice that will play a significant part in determining your future happiness. As you all are probably aware, what we do here at Mercy Clinic is the same thing that the smaller clinics do—

ANONYMOUS *(interrupting):* Perform abortions.

(A few of the women turn to look at her, some perhaps critically, some painfully.)

DIRECTOR: Yes, well, as I was saying, what we do here is the same as the smaller facilities do, but on a much larger scale. We are now equipped to treat as many as three dozen patients at one time. Why keep the customer waiting, we always say. In other words, you've made your choice, let's get on with it. *(Turns to* ASSISTANT*)* So, toward that end, my colleague, Terri, will be reading—

ASSISTANT *(interrupting):* Kerri.

DIRECTOR: Pardon me?

ASSISTANT: My name is Kerri. You said Terri.

DIRECTOR: Did I? I'm so sorry. My colleague Terri—

ASSISTANT: Kerri.

DIRECTOR: Kerri! *(Laughs)* We'll get it right one of these times! Terri will be reading off your names from the sign-in sheet and what I'd like for you to do is, as your name is called, please exit through the doorway behind me and go down the hallway to the reception area where a team of doctors and nurses will assist you in preparing for the, uh *(glances at* ANONYMOUS*)*—will assist you with all the necessary preparations. *(To* ASSISTANT*)* Terri?

ASSISTANT *(giving her a look):* Well, first of all, my name is Kerri, and your names, according to this list, are Maria van Bee—*(she mispronounces the name on her clipboard)* Maria van Beeth-a-ven?

(One of the women rises. It is MARIA.*)*

MARIA: Beethoven. Maria van Beethoven. It's German.

*(*MARIA *crosses past the* DIRECTOR *and her* ASSISTANT *and will exit through designated doorway.)*

ASSISTANT: Sorry. *(Reads, mispronounces)* Justyna Chop—

JUSTYNA *(rises):* Chopin. Justyna Chopin. It's Polish.

*(*JUSTYNA *crosses and exits.)*

ASSISTANT: Thank you. *(Reads)* Mary Washington.

(A third woman rises and exits. As each of the following names is called, another woman rises and exits. There should, of course, be a long enough pause between the reading of the names to provide not only ample opportunity for each of the women to exit but for the historical significance of each name to be grasped by the audience.)

Jane Jefferson
Nancy Lincoln
Hannah G. Grant
A Mrs. Eisenhower?
Jennie Churchill
Sara Roosevelt
Nancy Edison
Eliza Bell
Mary Ford
Susan Wright

(SUSAN *rises and walks with her head down toward doorway. As she does so, she is addressed by the* DIRECTOR.)

DIRECTOR: Back again, I see.

(SUSAN *halts momentarily, casts a glance at* DIRECTOR, *then hurries toward exit.*)

ASSISTANT: Amy Earhart
Pauline Einstein
Fanny Nightingale
Mrs. Pasteur
Dora Salk
Sarah Barton
Alberta King *(A black woman rises and exits.)*
Leona Parks *(A second black woman exits.)*
Mallie Robinson *(A third black woman exits.)*
Lucy Anthony

(ASSISTANT *struggles with next name.*)

Taissa Sol, Solzh—*(She looks to women for help.* TAISSA *rises.)*

TAISSA: Solzhenitzsyn. *(Smiles)* Russian.

(TAISSA *exits through designated doorway.* ASSISTANT *smiles cordially at her, resumes reading.*)

ASSISTANT: Rosa . . . oh boy. *(Looks up)* I'm sorry. I'm not very good at Yugoslavian names, either. Rosa?

ROSA *(rising):* Rosa Bojaxhiu.

ASSISTANT: Thank you.

(ROSA, *who has remained unseen until now if possible, begins crossing toward exit. In dress and stature she bears a resemblance to Mother Teresa.*)

ASSISTANT *(reading):* Katherine Keller
Hannah Chaplin
Flora Disney
Mrs. DiMaggio

Mrs. ten Boom
Betsey Moody
Morrow Graham
[Name of your pastor's or group leader's mother.]
Well—that's it.

(She has turned to address Director, *who has noticed* Anonymous *still sitting.)*

Director: Except for her.

Assistant: Oh. *(Checks her list)* Did I miss somebody?

Director *(to* Anonymous*)*: So what's your name?*

Anonymous *(quietly):* I don't have a name.

Assistant: I don't have any more names.

Director *(to* Anonymous*)*: Of course you do.

Assistant *(to* Director*)*: No, really. I checked them off as I read them.

Director: I mean her.

Assistant: Huh?

Director: She says she doesn't have a name.

Assistant: I thought everybody had a name.

Director: They do. Never heard of a single soul who didn't. Come on, girl, we don't have all day. What's your name?

Anonymous: Please. It would be so much easier without . . . naming names, don't you think?

Director: I'm sorry, but we have our rules. And you can't go in there without a name.

Anonymous: I can come out without a child, but I can't go in without a name. You people are really priceless.

Director: Hey, just give us a name and you're free to get on with the . . . procedure. A few minutes and it'll all be over.

Anonymous: Oh, that's where you're wrong. It'll never be over. All of history will echo with the sound of this "procedure."

Director *(becoming upset):* All right! Just give us a name, any name: Your favorite recipe, a city in Spain, I don't care. Just so we have something to put down on our page!

Anonymous: A line of poetry?

Director: What?

ANONYMOUS: Can I give you a line of poetry?

DIRECTOR: Fine. A line of poetry. Just so we have something to put down on the page.

ANONYMOUS *(with resolve):* "To be or not to be, that is the question."

ASSISTANT: That's poetry? It doesn't even rhyme.

DIRECTOR *(to* ASSISTANT*):* Just put it down. Let's get this over with. *(To* ANONYMOUS*)* How did that go again?

ANONYMOUS: "To be or not to be, that is the question."

(ASSISTANT *writes it down on list.)*

DIRECTOR: Can't say I've ever heard it before.

ANONYMOUS: That's because it was never written.

ASSISTANT: I don't understand.

ANONYMOUS: No. But his mother would.

ASSISTANT: Huh?

ANONYMOUS: Nothing. Nothing. *(Begins to exit, somberly)* Just put down Mrs. Nothing.

(The other two watch her go, then turn and begin to exit in another direction, their work finished for the time being. Lights fade out.)

Alternate Ending

(Insert at asterisk)

ANONYMOUS: Please. It would be so much easier without . . . naming names, don't you think?

DIRECTOR: I'm sorry, but we have our rules. And you can't go in there without a name.

ANONYMOUS: I can come out without a child, but I can't go in without a name. You people are really priceless.

DIRECTOR: Hey, just give us a name and you're free to get on with the . . . procedure. A few minutes and it'll all be over.

ANONYMOUS: Oh, that's where you're wrong. It'll never be over. All of history will echo with the sound of this "procedure."

DIRECTOR *(becoming upset)*: All right! Just give us a name, any name: Your favorite recipe, a city in Spain, I don't care. Just so we have something to put down on our page!

ANONYMOUS: Very well. Just put me down as Mary, please.

DIRECTOR *(to* ASSISTANT*)*: Did you get that? "Mary."

(ANONYMOUS *begins crossing to exit.)*

ASSISTANT *(writing):* Do you spell that M-A-R-Y or M-E-R-R-Y?

ANONYMOUS *(turning):* The first way. *(Troubled, speaking almost to herself)* Definitely the first way.

(ASSISTANT *finishes writing and* ANONYMOUS *continues her exit as lights fade out.)*

Pretty Nice View

Theme

The frenetic pace of modern life; the Sabbath rest

Tone

Farcical

Cast

MAN: *in a hurry*

WIFE: *in his wake*

BOY: *of any age, their son*

GIRL: *of any age, their daughter*

GANG: *of any age, number, or gender: their parents, siblings, cousins, neighbors—whatever. All dressed in colorful, outlandish beach clothing.*

Scene

A peaceful shoreline; empty stage will do.

Props

A variety of beach paraphernalia:

Cooler

Lawn chairs

Cots

Blankets

Towels

Umbrella

Skin diving equipment

Beach ball

Football

Inner tubes of all kinds

Beach bags

Boom box with loud, fast-paced music playing

Food items

Costumes

Beach clothes, as gaudy and humorous as possible.

Summary

Dad and the gang are ready for a day at the beach. They've got everything they need—beach towels, suntan lotion, radios, hot dogs—everything but time to enjoy the day. No sooner do they have things set up than it's time to head home.

(As sketch opens MAN *enters wearing gaudy beach garb. He looks frantically for an empty spot on the beach. Finding one center stage, he whistles and then motions several times for his offstage family to hurry up.)*

MAN: Come on—let's get a move on! We haven't got all—Oh, for Pete's sake. *(Rushes over to help his* WIFE, *who enters struggling with an overflowing armload of beach equipment: cooler, lawn chairs, etc. They bring these things center stage and begin setting up.)* We'd better get those hot dogs cooking right away. We don't have all—*(Looks offstage again)* Hurry up, you guys! Let's get set up here! *(Motions again)*

WIFE *(looking around):* How can I cook the hot dogs? There's no grill.

MAN: Yes there is—I saw one just up the beach, half a mile or so. Coals are still hot. If you hurry, you can claim it before anyone else does. *(As* WIFE *heads off)* Be careful—don't burn the buns!

*(*WIFE *has wearily picked up a cooler and is heading back the way she came, being bumped into and twirled around by the rest of the gang. They are carrying a variety of beach paraphernalia: cots, blankets, umbrella, skin diving equipment, beach ball, football, inner tubes of all kinds, towels, beach bags, and boom box with some loud, fast-paced music on it. They proceed to set up while* MAN *fusses and fumes.)*

MAN *(toward audience):* Hey, you guys, I thought I told you only five of you on the jet ski at once! *(Looks around)* Martha? *(To* BOY) Where's your mother?

BOY: I think I saw her heading off that way, muttering something about burnt buns. And the electric chair being worth the satisfaction, something like that.

MAN: Well, go tell her to hurry up. We don't have all—Hey! Where's the portable TV set? [*Or:* How come this TV isn't working?]

GIRL: Forgot to bring it, Dad. Sorry. [*Or:* Batteries are dead, I guess.]

MAN: Well, how in the world are we supposed to watch the ball game? For Pete's sake, what're we s'posed to do? Sit around lookin' at—that? *(Motions toward audience)* What *is* that, anyway?

GIRL *(looking toward audience)*: It's called: a scenic view. *(Pointing)* You've gotcher lake, you've gotcher trees, you've gotcher mountains in the background—

MAN *(busy with something)*: Yeah, yeah, whatever. *(To others)* Hey, we better hurry and get that volleyball net set up! We don't have all—

BOY *(entering)*: Mom says the hot dogs will be ready in about—

MAN *(looking at wristwatch)*: Oh no! Look at the time! Come on people, we gotta get a move on or we won't be back in time for—Hey, you guys, bring it on in! *(This last is to the group riding the jet ski)* We gotta scramble!

(Scramble they do: all onstage quickly rise and begin picking things up for a hasty exit.)

GIRL: But, Dad, aren't we gonna stay and watch the sunset?

MAN *(stopping momentarily)*: The what—? *(She points toward water; he waves her off.)* Ahh—happens every day! You can catch the rerun. Let's go, people!

(GIRL shakes her head, grabs a couple of chairs, and exits with everyone else. After a few seconds, WIFE enters, carrying the cooler and a plate of hot dogs. She looks around, sees no one, shrugs and sits down on cooler.)

WIFE: Hmmm, pretty nice view . . .

(Gazing toward audience, she takes a bite out of a hot dog as lights fade out.)

The Untouchables

(Is There Room in Your Church for Me?)

Theme

Brotherly love; acceptance; forgiveness

Tone

Serious

Cast

WOMAN-WITHOUT-EXCUSES
MAN-WITHOUT-DEFENSES
WOMAN-WITHOUT-A-FRIEND
MAN-WITHOUT-A-FUTURE
WOMAN-WITH-A-PAST
MAN-WITH-A-SECRET

Scene

An empty stage

Props

Purse
Whiskey bottle (half pint)
Baggie with white powder
Bottle of prescription pills

Costumes

Modern

Production Notes

The following monologues are independent of one another and therefore may be presented, with the exception of the final speaker, in any order desired. You may also wish to omit one or more of the monologues—again, with the exception of the final piece.

Summary

Six individuals with various problems and backgrounds address the congregation, asking whether there is room among them for the kind of individual each happens to be (i.e., will you love and accept me here despite my past or despite my problems?) A divorcé, a man dying of AIDS, an addict, a widower, a woman who has had an abortion, and a man with a secret identity each in turn steps onto the stage looking for a place to call "home."

(At rise the stage is in darkness. All actors sit or stand onstage, awaiting their turn to speak. The spotlight comes up on one person at a time, beginning with a soft-spoken woman in her late 30s or early 40s.)

WOMAN-WITHOUT-EXCUSES: It didn't work out—what more can I say?

I had my reasons, so did he.

I grew up believing divorce was wrong, except in cases of unfaithfulness, so did he.

Other women seem to have better excuses than I do: their husbands cheated on them, ran off with another woman, came home drunk and beat them up.

I can't claim any of that.

I wanted to have an ideal marriage, so did he.

We'd both been thinking the same thing the past few years: we'd both been wishing the other one would be unfaithful so that we'd have a legitimate biblical excuse to get a divorce.

I finally realized what a mockery of marriage that was.

And so did he.

And so, here I am, alone. I still need a church, I still need to feel a part of a community of believers, I still need love and acceptance and opportunities to participate and grow.

(She looks into the distance.)

And somewhere out there . . . so does he.

(Lights fade on her and come up on a thin, emaciated man in his late 30s or early 40s. There is bitterness in him, but its origin is rejection.)

MAN-WITHOUT-DEFENSES: I'm dying of AIDS—so don't get too close!

(Takes a few threatening steps toward audience, then smiles scornfully and retreats into spotlight)

I say that facetiously because I know that once you know that I have AIDS, you *won't* get close to me: geographically or emotionally.

Even though—even though the medical community has made it abundantly clear that you can't get AIDS from—from a handshake, or a hug, or a conversation, or from acceptance and love—even though everybody knows this, it's interesting to see how they keep their distance anyway.

And the irony—listen to this—the irony is that *I'm* in more danger of dying from what *you've* got than *you* are of dying from what *I've* got!

Did you hear what I just said?

You can't get AIDS from me—from talking with me or walking with me or from being my friend, but the viruses and germs that you share with me through a handshake or a hug or from just being in the same room with me are potentially far more disastrous to *me* than my friendship can ever be to you.

That virus that you bring into my vicinity may prove to be the one that my deficient immune system can't handle.

Or the one that wears me down just a little bit more and leaves me all the more vulnerable to the next exposure.

So please, don't consider friendship with me a fatal experience.

And here—here is the real irony.

Despite that, despite the fact that you carry death with you, despite the fact that your presence in my life might prove deadly for me, I still need that presence.

I still need your friendship.

Because as much as I'm dying of a deficiency in my immune system, I'm also dying of a deficiency of love.

I have AIDS.

Don't get too close.

(Lights fade on him and come up on a woman in her 20s or 30s. Her hair is greasy; her clothes are dirty. She harbors no grudges, only pain.)

WOMAN-WITHOUT-A-FRIEND: My name is—

(Sniffs, wipes her nose with her hand, coughs)

My name is Linda. And these—

(Sniffs again as she reaches into her handbag and pulls out a half pint of whiskey, a bag containing white powder, a bottle of prescription medication.)

79

These are my best friends.

(Tries to set the liquor down and spills the pills noisily all over the floor. Sets every-thing down.)

I'd really, really like to make some *new* friends.
Is there room in your church for me?

(Lights fade on her and come up on a man in his late 70s, unkempt, distracted. He is sitting in a rocking chair.)

MAN-WITHOUT-A-FUTURE: I'm feeling kind of dizzy after eating.
My doctor thinks it's just stress; he says I'm worrying too much.
I wake up early, start thinking, either about my wife in the nursing home or my brother in the hospital—tubes in his nose, semicomatose, can't breathe by himself.
If it was me I'd tell 'em to just pull the plug.

(A brief amount of time elapses.)

My wife, she's not coming back.
Diabetes.
She can only see this far in front of her face.

(Holds his hand eight inches in front of his face)

We've been together 56 years.
I've hardly ever been alone.
Sometimes I say something to the empty couch.
Sometimes I cough, early in the morning, and I try to control it so's not to wake her up.
Then I realize she's not there.

(A brief amount of time elapses.)

Don't drive anymore, I get confused.
Not all the time, just once in a while I forget where I am.
So I don't see her very much.
I call her three times a day: 8:30 after breakfast, 1:30 after lunch, 6:30 after dinner.
Ask her how she's feeling, what she had to eat, and if anyone came to visit her.
Mostly just to let each other know that we're still alive.

(Lights fade out on him and come up on a woman in her late teens or early 20s. At first her eyes are cold, her words icy.)

WOMAN-WITH-A-PAST: It wasn't rape.
It wasn't incest.
I was curious about sex, and I was crazy about Robert—
And I got careless.

And I got pregnant.

And then . . . I got an abortion.

I wish for your sakes I was in a more defensible position because maybe if it *had* been rape or incest—well, maybe then it would have somehow seemed more justifiable, or acceptable, or something.

But like I said, it wasn't.

It wasn't rape, and it wasn't incest.

It was pure and simple, clear-cut, premeditated—abortion.

It was something that I know many of you, if not all of you, consider wrong, and that I consider wrong in retrospect, but I can't undo it.

So you're just gonna have to live with it.

You're just gonna have to live with it—

(She breaks down, delivering the remainder of her lines through tears.)

Because I'm having trouble living with myself—

And I need to know there's somewhere I can go and feel loved and accepted no matter what I've done—

Somewhere I can go to start life over again—because I'd like to do it right this time.

I'd like to have a second chance.

Is there room in your church for me?

(Lights fade on her and come up on a man in his late 20s. He is somewhat withdrawn, hesitant, and speaks in a quiet, polite manner throughout.)

MAN-WITH-A-SECRET: My name—well, I guess that's not important for the moment.

What *is* important is that I feel that it's time.

Time that I came out of the closet.

After all, this seems to be the age of self-disclosure and revelation.

I know that there are those who prefer to live in denial, who can't bring themselves to risk rejection, but I feel I have no choice: I must be true to who I really am, no matter what the cost.

(Takes a deep breath)

I don't recall just when I began to realize . . . the truth about myself; it was more or less a gradual discovery, although there was an incident when I was about 12 years old that stands out in my memory.

I guess I knew it then, although at the time I certainly didn't understand the full implications of my . . . discovery.

But I won't go into all that right now.

The important thing—

The important thing is that it's time . . . time that I . . . came forward and told you, all of you, the truth about myself.

I know that some of the things I have to say will disturb some people—disturb them quite a bit, I'm afraid.

But I can't change what I am.

I can't be something I'm not.

So I've decided to come clean, as it were, and face the consequences, good or bad.

If you choose to reject me, well, so be it: That's the price a person pays for being who they are, of revealing to the world one's true identity.

So I come before you today as myself, my true self.

Whether or not you are comfortable with me, whether or not you can accept me, I am who I am and I cannot compromise that reality.

My name is Jesus Christ.

I have come to demonstrate the love of God.

Is there room in your church for Me?

(He looks out over the audience as the lights come up quickly but dimly on the stationary figures around him onstage, then fade out entirely.)

Tongues Afire: Cheapening the Name of God

Theme

Misusing God's name; the subtleties of temptation

Tone

Humorous

Cast

Male roles:
- FAHRENHEIT
- NAT KING COAL
- CINDER ELLIS
- RALPH WALDO EMBERSON (*optional; nonspeaking part*)

Female roles:
- ASHLEY
- SINTHIA
- BURNADETTE
- BLAZE (*optional; nonspeaking part*)

Scene

An office in hell

Props

Books
Piece of paper
Pens and notebooks
File cabinet or desk with drawers (optional)
Chairs
Couches
Coffee tables as desired

Costumes

Noncombustible!

Summary

A strategy team from down under has been given a difficult assignment: find a way to trick Homo sapiens into violating the third commandment. The team solves their problem by utilizing the age-old techniques they learned back in Lie School.

(As sketch begins ASHLEY *is standing off to one side, sulking. The rest of the cast, exhibiting postures and expressions of weariness and dejection, sit on chairs or couches, notebooks and pens nearby.)*

SINTHIA *(wearily):* Come on, Ashley. You may as well join the party.

ASHLEY *(sarcastic):* Right. *(Flops in chair)* Can you believe the nerve of that guy? Five nights in a row! How long is this going to continue?

FAHRENHEIT: Until we come up with a strategy that he'll accept.

ASHLEY: There *is* no strategy! Not this time. Nothing is gonna work. Doesn't he realize that? We've been at it for three months now and nothing. What's another all-nighter going to accomplish?

NAT KING COAL: She's right. You'd think after the great job we did on the other nine he'd ease up a bit, cut us some slack. *(They mutter their agreement.)*

BURNADETTE: Who does he think he is, anyway—God?

(Silence for several seconds as all turn their heads to face her, looks of superiority on their faces)

FAHRENHEIT *(serious):* That's *exactly* what he thinks. I mean, that's what the whole thing is about, right?

BURNADETTE: Oh yeah, I forgot. (*Grins sheepishly; shrugs*)

CINDER ELLIS: Hey, you guys, we really shouldn't be talking about him like this, should we? What if he's got the whole place bugged and he can hear everything we're saying?

ASHLEY: What's he gonna do, *punish* us? (*Laughter*) Add 10 years to our sentence? (*Louder laughter*) Like those prison terms on earth: *Life* plus 30 years! (*Feigns horror*) Eternity plus *10 years!* (*Howls of laughter*)

NAT KING COAL: Wow! *That'll* keep me in line!

BURNADETTE: Hey, that reminds me. You guys heard the one about the man who arrives at the Pearly Gates and a coupla angels come out—

OTHERS (*suddenly very serious*): Heard it!

FAHRENHEIT: Well, the sooner we get started the sooner we'll be done.

SINTHIA: *That's* profound.

ASHLEY: It's also a lie, because no matter *when* we get started, we're never gonna get done cuz there's nothing we can *do* with this one. Our goose is cooked.

NAT KING COAL: She's right. We're really in hot water this time.

ASHLEY: *Boiling* water. (*They laugh again.*)

BURNADETTE: Why don't we just go on strike?

(*Silence for several seconds as all again turn toward her*)

FAHRENHEIT (*serious*): To whom else would we go? He has the words of eternal night.

BURNADETTE: Oh yeah, I forgot.

SINTHIA: You know, it can't be that difficult. There's got to be some angle that we haven't thought about yet, something we're overlooking. (*Grabs a paper, reads with frustration*) Thou shalt not misuse the name of the Lord your God, for the Lord will not hold anyone guiltless who misuses his name. (*Stops reading*) There's got to be a handle somewhere, some way to trip 'em up.

ASHLEY: Well, he's not satisfied with any approach we've come up with so far.

FAHRENHEIT (*dejected*): So we're back at square one . . .

SINTHIA (*the light dawning*): Yes. (*Pause*) Yes!

ASHLEY: What? *What?*

SINTHIA: Square one. (*They look on, uncomprehending.*) Back to basics. (*They continue to stare.*) We forgot about the Big Three!

(All fall to the floor, cowering and covering their ears.)

ALL: Not *them!* The *Big Three Rules to Successful Temptation Strategy!*

(She begins tearing through drawers or piles of books and magazines.)

SINTHIA: Remember back in Lie School how Professor Burns used to screech at us that if we ever ran into problems we should always go back to the "Big Three"? *(Finds book)* Here it is! *(Opens it) Chapter 1.* Remember the title? "K-I-S-S"? *(Collective groan of recognition)*

ASHLEY *(painfully):* All together now—

OTHERS: Keep It Subtle, Stupid.

SINTHIA *(confirming):* Yes. Keep It Subtle, Stupid. *(Reads instructively, trying to fire them up)* Section 1: Subtlety Is a More Certain Sabotage. *(Stops reading)* And here—I've got this paragraph underlined: *(Reads again)* "It is conceivable that many of the humans will find a way to avoid committing the big and famous sins, at least for a time. *Your* job, while waiting and hoping for the potential *major* blunder, is to *corrode their souls* in subtle and unsuspected ways. *Remember: rust, too, is a form of fire.*" *(Stops reading; turns pages)* On to Chapter 2. Ah, remember the Triple-T formula? Temptation Takes Time? Here you go *(reads):* "It may actually be advantageous to allow an entire generation of humans to experience salvation *(others groan, cover their ears for a moment)—if within that generation* you are able to plant the seeds that will grow up to *choke and strangle* many generations to come. So, first find a subtle, almost unnoticeable approach, and then second, take your time that it might: infiltrate, marinate, annihilate—"

OTHERS *(chanting):* Infiltrate—marinate—annihilate!

(They repeat this at least three more times, perhaps even rising and parading around the room, caught up in the revered strategies of destruction that are so dear to their hearts.)

SINTHIA: OK, OK, OK. *(They settle down.)* So we need something they won't notice—something subtle that will corrode them over time, possibly over many centuries—from generation to generation.

ASHLEY: But *what?*

SINTHIA *(turns pages, reads):* Chapter 3: The Art of Cheapening. "All that is sacred must be made common and crude. Anything and everything that reflects eternal values must be diminished and demeaned lest its true worth be understood and cherished." *(Stops reading)* Remember what we did to sex?

OTHERS *(general uproar):* Yahoo! Wooooo! Yee-ha! *(Etc.)*

BURNADETTE *(rising, hands raised):* Hallelujah! *(Sudden silence as OTHERS turn and glare; she puts hand to her mouth in sudden horror.)* Woops—sorry. Wrong word. *(Sits down again, embarrassed)*

ASHLEY: OK. So what we're supposed to do, according to your book there, is to find a subtle way to gradually, over time, cheapen something sacred until it seems irrelevant and worthless. But how in the world are we gonna *do* that with the name of God? It's totally revered by the humans: It's "Praise-God-for-this," "Praise-God-for-that," "Did-you-see-what-God-did-here?" "Did-you-see-what-He-created-there?" "Listen-how-God-helped-me-with-this," "I'm-trusting-God-to-provide-me-with-that." *Every time they mention His name*, it's associated with something *positive*— (*She freezes mid-thought; the light has dawned. The* OTHERS *look up from their notebooks, etc.*) So we connect it with something *negative!* Get them to use His name when things go wrong!

NAT KING COAL (*with British accent*): By jove, I think she's got it! Every time they make a mistake, lose their way—

FAHRENHEIT: Fall down or, or bump their head—

ASHLEY: Get some bad news, even something minor—

SINTHIA: Hit their thumb with a hammer—

(OTHERS *laugh and cheer this one.*)

ASHLEY: Every time they lose a ball game—

BURNADETTE: Or lose the ball—

(OTHERS *laugh kindly over this offering of hers.*)

CINDER ELLIS: Or get a bad call from the referee—

(OTHERS *ooh and aah over this one.*)

ASHLEY: They'll be mentioning God's name. They'll be connecting His name with so many frustrating, piddling, meaningless situations that it'll lose all other significance! Well, probably not for everyone, but for *some*. For *many. Enough* of them.

(*The* OTHERS *look at her, look around at each other, smiling.*)

FAHRENHEIT: I think she just solved our problem. What do you all say? I propose a toast.

NAT KING COAL: *Burnt*, preferably. A *burnt* toast!

FAHRENHEIT (*begins singing*): For she's a jolly good devil—

OTHERS (*joining in, also singing*): For she's a jolly good devil, / for she's a jolly good devil / witch nobody can deny!

(*They have tossed their pens and notebooks into the air and have begun exiting, marching toward the main office. Perhaps they carry* ASHLEY *on their shoulders, perhaps they fly. In any case, they probably continue singing on the way out as lights fade to black.*)

Something Old, Something New, Sometimes Even Something Blue

Theme

Marriage

Tone

Humorous with a serious aspect

Cast

DAUGHTER: *a woman in her early 20s*
MOTHER: *a woman in her late 40s*
GRANDMA: *a woman in her early 70s*

Scene

A living room

Props

Ironing board
Iron
Laundry basket

Clean laundry
Ironed clothes on hangers
Engagement ring
Easy chair

Costumes

Modern

Production Notes

It is suggested that this play be followed by a sermon and/or discussion on the subject of love and marriage, addressing not only the tendency to romanticize the past and the future, but also the struggles facing those who find themselves stuck in a relationship that seems to have lost the luster and the joy one is led to expect.

Summary

A 20-year-old daughter arrives home excited to share with her visiting grandmother the news of her recent engagement. As she goes on and on enthusiastically about the expected bliss of her upcoming marriage, her 45-year-old mother (in the midst of a half ton of ironing) offers her own skeptical comments about her daughter's remarks. Likewise, the grandmother, a 75-year-old widow rocking gently in a chair, reflects on the subject at hand, from wedding vows to snoring, from table manners to the division of labor in the home. Thus three generations take turns commenting on the idealistic expectations, bittersweet realities, and poignant memories of that arrangement to end all arrangements—marriage.

(*As the scene begins, the* MOTHER *is working wearily at an ironing board stage right and the* GRANDMA *is dozing contentedly in an easy chair stage left. Although their places onstage might change briefly, these are their basic positions throughout the scene. The* GRANDMA *awakes moments after the lights come up.*)

GRANDMA: Ooh. Hum. Is she here yet?

MOTHER: Any minute now, Mom.

GRANDMA: I seem to have dozed off for a second.

MOTHER: An hour and a half, actually.

GRANDMA: Was it that long?

MOTHER: All of *Rikki,* half of *Oprah.*

GRANDMA: Did I miss anything?

(MOTHER *holds a shirt up, turns it over.)*

MOTHER: Same old stuff. Dirty laundry, trash pickup, junk male.

GRANDMA: I meant the talk shows.

MOTHER: So did I.

GRANDMA: Oh. *(Looks around)* I thought she would be here by now.

MOTHER: She will, Mom. She can't wait to tell you.

GRANDMA: The exciting news.

MOTHER: Yeah. The exciting news.

GRANDMA: *You* don't seem too excited about it, though.

MOTHER: Well, I'm tired, Mom. First of all, she kept me up talking about her exciting news till half past 11:00, then George decided to keep me up till half past 2:00.

GRANDMA: How romantic.

MOTHER: Not really. He was snoring.

GRANDMA: Oh.

MOTHER: You know what a light sleeper I am.

GRANDMA: Why didn't you try the couch?

MOTHER: I was *on* the couch. That man's snore could attract a romantic moose . . .

GRANDMA: Oh, come now.

MOTHER: From Canada.

GRANDMA: Oh—the way you talk.

MOTHER: He's not as bad as Dad was though, thank heavens.

GRANDMA: Your father wasn't a snorer.

MOTHER: Mom—he used to drown out Johnny Carson.

GRANDMA: Well, yes, he did have a habit of dozing off in front of the television set.

MOTHER: No—from the bedroom. With the door closed. If Carson didn't speak in between Dad's inhalations, we'd miss the entire punch line.

GRANDMA: You're exaggerating and you know it.

MOTHER: And you're suffering from selective memory loss.

GRANDMA: From what?

MOTHER: You always make being married to Dad sound like a bed of roses.

(The older woman smiles to herself.)

GRANDMA: He used to buy me one twice a week.

MOTHER: A bed?

GRANDMA: A rose. Every Tuesday and Friday on the way home from work. Told people it was a good business investment. The rose would put *me* in a good mood, I in turn would put *him* in a good mood, and he would then put his *customers* in a good mood, which in turn increased his sales.

MOTHER: Mom, he sold cement. There's only so much a person needs. What, do you think his customers went home and said, Guess what, dear, we're gonna concrete the living room—Fred was in such a good mood I bought extra?

GRANDMA: Well, I don't know, but it was nice getting those three roses every week.

MOTHER: *Two* roses, Mom.

GRANDMA: Yes, every Monday and Thursday.

MOTHER: You said Tuesday and Friday.

GRANDMA: Yes.

DAUGHTER *(offstage):* Hello! Mom?

MOTHER *(holding up the iron):* In here, Susan, playing house.

DAUGHTER *(entering):* Is she here yet?

MOTHER: Why don't you ask her?

DAUGHTER: Grandma!

GRANDMA: Oh, Sweetheart!

(Hugs and all that)

DAUGHTER: Sorry I'm late. My lab went extra long.

GRANDMA: Lab? Now what class is that for?

DAUGHTER: Biology.

MOTHER: More like chemistry, I suspect.

DAUGHTER: *Mom. (Gives her* MOTHER *a mildly annoyed look)* You didn't tell her, did you? Grandma, did she say anything?

GRANDMA: Nothing of interest.

DAUGHTER: OK. Sit down.

GRANDMA: My normal position. *(She sits.)*

DAUGHTER: You know Greg.

GRANDMA: Yes—

DAUGHTER: Well, OK, last night he took me to *Oklahoma*—

GRANDMA: And you're back already?

DAUGHTER: What—?

MOTHER: Not the state, Mom. The play.

GRANDMA: Oh.

DAUGHTER: *Oklahoma.* My favorite musical. Over at West High. Afterward we went for a walk down near Lexington—

GRANDMA: Kentucky?

DAUGHTER: No—Lexington Avenue. With all the big trees I like so much? And we came to my favorite oak tree, it's really huge, and there's this knothole about shoulder high—

GRANDMA: Uh-huh.

DAUGHTER: Just like *To Kill a Mockingbird.*

GRANDMA: You do?

DAUGHTER: What?

GRANDMA: Like to kill a mockingbird—

MOTHER: The *movie*, Mom. Remember Gregory Peck?

GRANDMA: Oh, *that* Gregory. I thought you meant your *boyfriend*—

DAUGHTER: I *do.* *(Seeking support)* Mom?

MOTHER: *Mom*, in the movie with Gregory Peck there was a knothole in the tree and his kids kept finding little treasures in it.

GRANDMA: Oh, yes.

DAUGHTER: Anyway, Greg tells me—*my* Gregory—to reach inside the knothole to see if I find anything and I said, No way, Jose, it might be occupied by a—

GRANDMA: A mockingbird?

DAUGHTER: Who *knows* what. So he finally convinces me it's safe, and I reach inside and there's a box that his friends had put in there just a few minutes before and guess what it was!

GRANDMA: A box!

MOTHER: *Inside,* Mom. *Inside* the box.

GRANDMA: I haven't the faintest—(DAUGHTER *exhibits diamond ring on left hand.)* Oh, my! Oh—how beautiful! (*More hugs and all that.* MOTHER *looks on, smiling but restrained.)* I knew it the moment your mother said you had some exciting news to tell me. She's excited, too, but your father kept her up half the night.

DAUGHTER (*looks at* MOTHER *with raised eyebrows):* How romantic.

MOTHER: He snored.

DAUGHTER: Oh. Again? I thought you bought earplugs.

MOTHER: I did. I stuffed them up his nose. Didn't help a bit.

GRANDMA: So—when is the wedding?

DAUGHTER: We're not sure. We think May or June.

GRANDMA (*reflective):* Roger and I were married in June. Lovely, lovely day.

MOTHER: Mom, there was a tornado, a flood, and an earthquake.

GRANDMA: Yes, I do seem to remember it being slightly overcast. So, where is he going to take you on your honeymoon?

DAUGHTER (*with a twinkle in her eye):* We're not sure yet, but Greg's been hinting at the South Pacific.

GRANDMA: The musical?

DAUGHTER: The ocean—

MOTHER: Hawaii, Mom.

GRANDMA: I think I read that. Michener.

MOTHER: No, Mom, that was *Alaska.*

GRANDMA: Oh, well then I must have read it *in* Hawaii.

DAUGHTER: Hey, could you two stop with the book reviews already? I'm getting married—it's not something a girl does every day, you know.

MOTHER: No—once every 70 years is enough.

(DAUGHTER *gives her a look, confused.)*

GRANDMA: I'm sure the two of you will be as happy as Roger and I were. Now tell me all about him. Is this the tall curly-haired boy who plays basketball?

DAUGHTER: *Basketball?*

MOTHER: That's her *brother,* Mom. My *son,* your *grandson.*

DAUGHTER: You met him last Easter, Grandma—don't you remember?

GRANDMA: Ah.

DAUGHTER: He *is* tall, though.

GRANDMA: Your grandfather always stood head and shoulders above all the others.

(*Lost in a daze,* DAUGHTER *raises a hand above her head, imagining her boyfriend standing near her. She is standing center stage, her* MOTHER *and* GRANDMA *on either side, in their original spots. All three women maintain their positions for the remainder of the play as each reflects in her own way on the man in her life.*)

DAUGHTER: Taller than me by almost a foot.

MOTHER: Just so the foot stays out of his mouth.

DAUGHTER: He always says the nicest things.

GRANDMA: Roger would write me the most romantic letters.

MOTHER: George always yells so sweetly for something to eat.

DAUGHTER: He said it doesn't matter that I don't know much about cooking—we'd make meals a cooperative effort.

MOTHER: Yeah, we've had a cooperative effort when it comes to meals. I cook, he eats.

GRANDMA: Roger usually worked till 7:00, so I would have supper waiting. But he never failed to clear the table and help with dishes.

DAUGHTER: I'd be so lost without him.

MOTHER: Wait till the two of you take a trip together. That stopping-to-ask-for-directions thing?

GRANDMA: Roger and I would always say that we were on a road together going in the same direction, adjusting ourselves to each other's pace and progress.

DAUGHTER: I can't wait.

MOTHER: You can wait.

GRANDMA: We wanted to wait to get married, but with the war and everything . . .

DAUGHTER: A man's clothes hanging in the closet . . .

MOTHER: If he bothers to hang them up at all.

GRANDMA: I still have Roger's Air Force uniform hanging in the closet, and his Sunday suit . . .

DAUGHTER: He has the nicest voice, the darkest eyes . . .

GRANDMA: I think what I loved the most about him was how he always took the time to listen . . .

MOTHER (*flailing her arms*): I used to wonder why I'd always find myself gesturing like John Madden when I spoke to him, then I realized it was because John Madden and I were both talking to him at the same time. I never know what the score is, but I'm usually fairly certain about who's wining the play-by-play.

DAUGHTER: We're going to write our own vows.

GRANDMA: Nobody thought about writing their own vows back then, but it wouldn't have made any difference what we said. Our hearts were committed forever, that's all that mattered.

DAUGHTER: Well, maybe we'll write our own but keep the traditional ones as well.

GRANDMA: For better—

MOTHER: For worse—

DAUGHTER: For richer—

MOTHER: For poorer—

GRANDMA: In sickness—

DAUGHTER: And in health—

EVERYONE: Till death do us part.

(*The lights fade out as the three women stare into the distance, holding in their respective gaze romance, reality, remembrance.*)